"This cookbook has some of the best recipes ever compiled.Wonderful layout—easy to read."
JIMMY HARRIS—President, Louisiana Bed and Breakfast Association

"Trusting a recipe often comes down to trusting the source. The sources for the recipes are impeccable; in fact, they're some of the best chefs in the nation."
BON APPETIT MAGAZINE

"Should be in the library—and kitchen—of every serious cook."
JIM WOOD—Food & Wine Editor—San Francisco Examiner

"A well-organized and user-friendly tribute to many of the state's finest restaurant chefs."
SAN FRANCISCO Chronicle

"An attractive guide to the best restaurants and inns, offering recipes from their delectable repertoire of menus."
GAIL RUDDER KENT—Country Inns Magazine

"Outstanding cookbook"
HERITAGE NEWSPAPERS

"I couldn't decide whether to reach for my telephone and make reservations or reach for my apron and start cooking."
JAMES MCNAIR—Best-selling cookbook author

"It's an answer to what to eat, where to eat—and how to do it yourself."
THE MONTEREY HERALD

"I dare you to browse through these recipes without being tempted to rush to the kitchen."
PAT GRIFFITH—Chief, Washington Bureau, Blade Communications, Inc.

Books of the "Secrets" Series

LOUISIANA'S

GUIDEBOOK & COOKBOOK

COOKING SECRETS

Kathleen DeVanna Fish

BON VIVANT

Library of Congress Cataloging-in-Publication Data

Louisiana's Cooking Secrets
The Chefs' Secret Recipes
Fish, Kathleen DeVanna
97-071560
ISBN 1-883214-16-5
$15.95 softcover
Includes indexes
Autobiography page

Copyright ©1998 by Kathleen DeVanna Fish
Cover photograph by Robert N. Fish
Editorial direction by Judie Marks
Cover design by Morris Design
Illustrations by Krishna Gopa, Graphic Design and Illustration
Interior photographs courtesy of Louisiana Department of State, Division of Archives,
    Records Management and History
Type by Cimarron Design

Published by Bon Vivant Press
a division of The Millennium Publishing Group
P.O. Box 1994
Monterey, CA 93942

Printed in the United States of America
by Publishers Press

Contents

Mardi Gras in New Orleans with Rex—King of Mardi Gras—on the float, toasting at Gallier Hall.

Photo from the Louisiana Department of State, Division of Archives, Records Management and History

Adventure into the Cuisines of Louisiana

Pirates and priests, gamblers and trappers, plantation ladies and voodoo queens: Louisiana has the most colorful history of any state and many countries. Spend the night in a haunted plantation, surrounded by cotton fields and family treasures. Plan a romantic rendezvous in the very bedroom that inspired a series of *Harlequin Romances*. Enjoy a home-cooked breakfast in a Cajun cottage and hear fascinating stories you'll remember for years. Let *Louisiana's Cooking Secrets* be your guide.

This is a very personal book. It offers you inside information on the best restaurants and inns—and it reveals the secret recipes of 58 of the greatest chefs in the state of Louisiana. Nobody paid to be included—the chefs and inns were hand-selected and invited to participate.

To help you get into the spirit of romance and adventure, the book is divided into five geographical zones: Recommended inns and restaurants—and their recipes—are listed for each zone, accompanied by tidbits of history, legend and lore. Plus we've added rare photographs that help you understand how Louisiana evolved.

Louisiana cuisine is a melting pot of diverse cultures, including French, Spanish, Italian, African, American Indian and Caribbean. This cookbook/guidebook explores the rich cooking heritage that resulted. We offer you recipes for beignets and crawfish bisque and jambalaya, shrimp rémoulade, pecan pie and red beans 'n rice. You will learn how to make elegant pompano en papillote, funky filé z'herbes, po-boy, chow-chow and gumbo. We ended up with a spectacular collection of secrets from the finest chefs highlighting what they cook, how they do it, their approaches and styles.

It was tempting to invite only the most famous chefs. While you will recognize many of the big names in this book, we have included some who may be new to you. The chefs provided 164 of their kitchen-tested secret recipes for the home cook. To make your life easier, we include preparation times and cooking times. Some of the recipes are simple. Some are more complex.

If you're going to make it yourself, you've got to have the right ingredients, so we included a mail-order resource guide. And because everything about Louisiana is unique, we added a dictionary and glossary to help you get around.

Louisiana's Cooking Secrets captures the flavors and spirit of the South. Prepare to be tempted.

Louisiana Restaurants and Inns

Sportsman's Paradise

Crossroads

Cajun Country

Plantation Country

Greater New Orleans

Chefs' Favorite Recipes

Breakfast and Breads

Appetizers

Soups

Salads

Seafood

Poultry

Meat and Alligator

Pasta and Grains

Vegetables and Side Dishes

Final Temptations

Cooking Stars of Louisiana

ALEX PATOUT'S LOUISIANA RESTAURANT

NEW ORLEANS

504 525-7788

Page 122

ANDREA'S

METAIRIE

504 834-8583

Page 128

ANTOINE'S

NEW ORLEANS

504 581-4422

Page 133

ARNAUD'S

NEW ORLEANS

504 523-5433

Page 137

BACCO

NEW ORLEANS

504 522-2426

Page 144

BELLA LUNA

NEW ORLEANS
504 529-1583
Page 148

BIZOU

NEW ORLEANS
504 524-4114
Page 154

BRIGTSEN'S

NEW ORLEANS
504 861-7610
Page 158

BROUSSARD'S

NEW ORLEANS
504 581-3866
Page 164

CAFÉ MILANO

HOUMA
504 879-2426
Page 56

CAFÉ VERMILIONVILLE
LAFAYETTE
318 237-0100
Page 62

CHARLEY G'S
METAIRIE
504 837-6408
Page 168

COMMANDER'S PALACE
NEW ORLEANS
504 899-8221
Page 174

G & E COURTYARD GRILL
NEW ORLEANS
504 528-9376
Page 178

GABRIELLE
NEW ORLEANS
504 948-6233
Page 183

GALATOIRE'S

NEW ORLEANS

504 525-2021

Page 187

GAUTREAU'S

NEW ORLEANS

504 899-7397

Page 191

JOE'S DREYFUS STORE

FORDOCHE

504 637-2625

Page 96

KELSEY'S

NEW ORLEANS

504 897-6722

Page 197

LA MADELEINE

NEW ORLEANS

504 861-8661

Page 201

LA PROVENCE

LACOMBE

504 626-7662

Page 205

LA RIVIERA

METAIRIE

504 888-6238

Page 209

LAFITTE'S LANDING

DONALDSONVILLE

504 473-1232

Page 100

MAISON LACOUR

BATON ROUGE

504 275-3755

Page 104

MIKE'S ON THE AVENUE

NEW ORLEANS

504 523-1709

Page 215

MONSIEUR PATOU

SHREVEPORT
318 868-9822
Page 31

MR. B'S BISTRO

NEW ORLEANS
504 523-2078
Page 219

PALACE CAFÉ

NEW ORLEANS
504 523-1661
Page 221

PERISTYLE

NEW ORLEANS
504 593-9535
Page 224

PREJEAN'S

LAFAYETTE
318 896-3247
Page 66

PRUDHOMME'S CAJUN CAFÉ

CARENCRO

318 896-7964

Page 70

RED FISH GRILL

NEW ORLEANS

504 523-6441

Page 228

SPORTSMAN'S PARADISE

CHAUVIN

504 594-2414

Page 74

UPPERLINE

NEW ORLEANS

504 891-9822

Page 232

The Regions of Louisiana

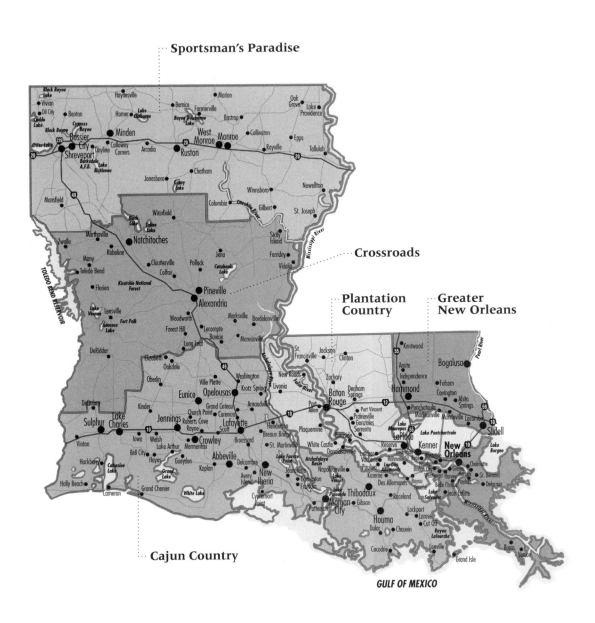

Sportsman's Paradise

Crossroads

Plantation Country

Greater New Orleans

Cajun Country

GULF OF MEXICO

Water, water everywhere—more than 7,500 miles of navigable waterways—the Mississippi, Ouachita and Red Rivers, giant lakes, such as Pontchartrain, great Bayous, (marshlands), all drain into the Gulf of Mexico. Louisiana is relatively flat. The highest point in the state, Driskill Mountain, is only 525 feet above sea level. Louisiana's culture is truly "different" from the rest of the nation—political subdivisions are measured by parishes rather than counties; while the rest of the country is based on British common law, the French Code Napoleon is the basis of law in Louisiana.

Although it all started with Spanish explorer Hernando de Soto, it was Robert Cavalier de La Salle who claimed the Louisiana territory for France in 1682. Twenty-five years later, the "real" history of Louisiana began with the founding of New Orleans. Louisiana Creoles, descendants of early French and/or Spanish settlers, were followed in 1755 by Acadians ("Cajuns"), French settlers in Nova Scotia, Canada, who were forcibly transferred by the British to Louisiana (an event commemorated in Longfellow's *Evangeline*). The Cajuns settled near Bayou Teche. Another group, the Islenos, Canary Islanders, were brought to Louisiana by a Spanish governor in 1770.

The next forty years were tumultuous indeed. Louisiana was a financial drain, so France ceded it to Spain in 1762; but when the expensive French and Indian War came to an end, Napoleon Bonaparte coerced Spain into giving it back in 1800. Only three years later, France needed money to fight yet another war against England, so it sold Louisiana to the young American government for $15 million. In 1812, Louisiana became the 18th state to enter the union, but in 1815, after the Treaty of Ghent had supposedly ended the War of 1812 between Britain and the United States, British forces invaded New Orleans. Andrew Jackson, with the help of Creoles, Choctaw Indians, slaves, pirates (including Jean Lafitte) and frontiersmen, soundly defeated the English, becoming a national hero and ultimately propelling himself into the White House.

From 1800 to 1860, Louisiana's population grew from 50,000 to 700,000, due to plantation agriculture. The Civil War, insects, poor weather and mechanization all but destroyed Louisiana's farm base. It was not until 1901, when the first oil well revealed the vast mineral resources of the State, that

LOUISIANA: Mardi Gras and a Whole Lot More

☆

Louisiana started to recover. But inept—or corrupt—politicians failed to tax profits and, as a result, the bounty of the petro-chemical industry went to northern corporations.

The years 1928 to 1935 marked the era of Huey "Kingfish" Long, the charismatic governor who was loved and vilified more than any other politician in the state's history. Although he exercised dictatorial power and corruption second to none, many said he would have been elected president of the United States had he not been felled by an assassin's bullet.

After World War II, petroleum and natural gas continued as Louisiana's greatest sources of wealth, but with the collapse of prices in the early 1980s, the state faced economic collapse and was saved only by a dramatic rise in tourism. Louisiana is the third-largest refiner of petroleum in the United States. It's rated among the top ten producers of sweet potatoes, sugar cane, rice, cotton, pecans and soybeans. More than a quarter of all seafood landed in the United States comes from Louisiana. New Orleans and Baton Rouge are among the five busiest ports in the United States. And then there's New Orleans—Dixieland, Bourbon Street and Mardi Gras...

Famous Louisianans include Louis Armstrong, Judah Philip Benjamin (Jewish treasurer of the Confederacy), Antoine "Fats" Domino, Pete Fountain, Al Hirt, Huey Long, Branford Marsalis, Winton Marsalis, Henry Miller and Paul Prudhomme.

Here are some of the highlights of a trip to Louisiana.

AVERY ISLAND, reached by a toll bridge, is underlaid by a great salt dome. The two primary attractions, one natural and one gastronomic, are the JUNGLE GARDENS, 200 acres of sub-tropical flora, sunken gardens, more than 20,000 herons, deer, alligators and a Chinese garden with a Buddha dating from 1,000 A.D., and the McIlhenny Company, which has been manufacturing Tabasco® brand red capsicum pepper sauce since 1868.

BATON ROUGE, Louisiana's capital, houses the STATE CAPITOL, constructed of marble from every marble-producing country in the world, and the LOUISIANA STATE UNIVERSITY RURAL LIFE MUSEUM, which re-creates an 1800s plantation.

CAJUN BAYOU COUNTRY is widespread. You can take Cajun swamp cruises in **HOUMA, KRAEMER, LAFAYETTE, JEAN LAFITTE, SLIDELL** and **WESTWEGO.** At Vermillion-ville, south of Lafayette, there's a 23-acre living history re- cre-

☆

ation of 17th and 18th century Cajun and Creole Louisiana. To savor the true flavor of Cajun Country, a trip to **ST. MARTINVILLE** is a must. Legends of Evangeline, the character created by Longfellow, proliferate. The EVANGELINE OAK, at the foot of Port Street, where Evangeline and her lover are said to have met, is said to be the most photographed tree in America. The LONGFELLOW-EVANGELINE STATE COMMEMORATIVE AREA, a 157-acre preserve bordering Bayou Teche, houses a large plantation and exhibits depicting Cajun life in the mid-19th century. ST. MARTIN DE TOURS CATHOLIC CHURCH, established in 1765, features a baptismal font donated by King Louis XVI and the grave of Emmeline Labiche, thought to be the heroine of Longfellow's *Evangeline.*

All roads lead to "The Big Easy"—**NEW ORLEANS,** whose very contradictions only add to its charm. Elegant brick and plaster buildings with gilded iron balconies stand in the shadow of soaring skyscrapers. Ocean-going liners dock adjacent to vegetable vendors selling produce from mule-drawn wagons. Unquestionably the heart of the City— the magnet that draws millions of visitors each year—is *Vieux Carré*—the FRENCH QUARTER. Typical of New Orleans' contradictions, the "French Quarter" is actually Spanish! Disastrous fires destroyed most of the original French buildings.

Legendary characters of yesteryear haunt the district. On Bourbon Street, near upper-crust Royal Street, Jean and Pierre Lafitte operated a fencing operation for their pirate contraband. Voodoo queen Marie Laveau frequented St. Louis Cathedral. Maspero's Exchange on Chartres Street was for years a hotbed of political intrigue, with would-be "liberators" constantly plotting the overthrow of revolution-ripe banana republics to the South. There's the BEAUREGARD-KEYES HOUSE, home to Confederate General Beauregard; the CABILDO STATE HOUSE, from which the Spanish governor ruled; the HERMANN-GRIMA HOUSE, a restored 1831 mansion with Creole kitchen, slave quarters and Creole cooking demonstrations; and, at the very heart of the French Quarter, JACKSON SQUARE, the Quarter's unofficial Left Bank. ST. LOUIS CATHEDRAL is one of the oldest (1794) and most photographed churches in the country. If you're a Wax Museum buff, you'll love the MUSEE CONTI WAX MUSEUM, with historically accurate settings covering New Orleans' history from 1699 to the present.

☆

If you don't stop in at PRESERVATION HALL, you may as well miss New Orleans altogether. Each night five or six bands take turns performing traditional jazz in its purest form. Expect to wait in line a long time, then stand through the entire performance. And expect to come out feeling it was well worth the wait and the discomfort!

New Orleans' dining and night life are legendary. The city is home to two authentic American cuisines—Cajun and Creole. Both come from French, Spanish and African kitchens. Creole originated in the French Quarter and Cajun cooking developed in the Bayou areas of the state. Cajun is traditionally hotter and heartier than Creole cuisine and is characterized by hot peppers, sausages and roux.

The city's reputation for nightlife began when the first women France sent to New Orleans quickly turned to the world's oldest profession. The raw frontier atmosphere welcomed them with open arms, as it were, and soon New Orleans was one of the pleasure capitals of the world. Storyville preached control rather than suppression. Today the "scandals" of another era are more nostalgic than actual, but watch yourself and your wallet on Bourbon Street, home of strip joints and sharks, where anything goes—including your money. Jazz was born in New Orleans and still forms the basis of The Big Easy's abundant nightlife, from Pete Fountain's Night Club in the New Orleans Hilton, to Preservation Hall.

The one event synonymous with New Orleans is MARDI GRAS. The actual Mardi Gras period is only the last third of Carnival Season (January 6 to Shrove Tuesday). In a sense, Mardi Gras lasts all year: the planning for next year's celebration begins just after Lent. There are parades, private balls and gaiety unmatched anywhere in the United States—the epitome of the Latin trait of total joyousness followed by total solemnity.

☆

If you like baseball, basketball, bass fishing and golf, Sportsman's Paradise is true to its name. Steeped in Southern tradition but coupled with modern progressiveness, Sportsman's Paradise offers activities ranging from bass fishing to ballet.

Grab your rod and reel and try your luck at any of the lakes, rivers and bayous. This community is brimming with jogging paths and nature trails, surrounded by tranquil lakes and acres of landscaped parks.

In **SHREVEPORT,** home of Blues great Huddy "Leadbelly" Ledbetter and the original Louisiana Hayride musical broadcasts, you'll find the second-largest airport in the state. Shreveport is also home of the R.W. NORTON ART GALLERY, featuring a private collection of Remingtons; the FAIRFIELD-HIGHLAND HISTORIC DISTRICT, the SPORTS MUSEUM OF CHAMPIONS and, of course, the LOUISIANA DOWNS thoroughbred racetrack in Bossier City.

In **RUSTON,** you can go on an old-fashioned hayride, attend a LOUISIANA PASSION PLAY or visit the world-renowned pottery at the ODELL POTTERY WORKSHOP.

Pay a visit to the MASUR MUSEUM in **MONROE,** the 2,000-figure REBECCA'S DOLL MUSEUM and the LOUISIANA PURCHASE GARDENS AND ZOO. Take a ride on the TWIN CITY QUEEN, a triple-decker boat that cruises up and down the Quachita River.

If you are looking for small-town Louisiana, travel to historic spots like **VIVIAN, JONESBORO, ARCADIA AND BASTROP.** Wander along Interstate 20 or follow the scenic byways to fascinating places like the GERMANTOWN MUSEUM in **MINDEN,** the BERNICE DEPOT MUSEUM in **BERNICE** or the CADDO-PINE ISLAND MUSEUM in **OIL CITY.**

Sportsman's Paradise

Contact:

Shreveport-Bossier Convention and Tourist Bureau
P.O. Box 1761
Shreveport, Louisiana 71166
(800) 551-8682
(318) 222-9391

Monroe/West Monroe Convention and Visitors Bureau
P.O. Box 6054
Monroe, Louisiana 71211-6054
(800) 843-1872
(318) 387-5691

Logging in Louisiana's pine forests.

Hunting in Sportsman's Paradise. In the center is Governor Jimmy Davis who penned the song "You Are My Sunshine."

Photos from the Louisiana Department of State, Division of Archives, Records Management and History

MONSIEUR PATOU

FRENCH
855 Pierremont Road
Shreveport, Louisiana 71106
(318) 868-9822
Dinner Monday–Saturday 6 p.m.–11 p.m.
Lunch Tuesday–Friday 11:30 a.m.–2 p.m.
AVERAGE DINNER FOR TWO: $120

There is a little bit of France in Shreveport. Tucked away in Towne Oak Square is Monsieur Patou, a special place distinguished by its exceptional elegance, comfortable setting and warm atmosphere. Add to that, the culinary talents of Chef Patou, and you are treated to an epicurean dining experience. Every ingredient is fresh and natural and the dishes are prepared from scratch.

The atmosphere is romantic, with soft lighting, peach-colored linens with fresh flowers, French china and fine silver. There is only one seating each night, so guests are encouraged to relax and enjoy the evening.

Menu appetizers include a delicate Cream Soup of Fresh English Peas with Country Ham and Croutons, a Fluffy Spinach Flan with Bacon and Fava Beans and a Hickory Smoked Salmon Salad served with a Cauliflower Vinaigrette. Entrees such as the Crispy Roasted Duck in Oriental Spices with an Orange and Cranberry Sauce and the best cut of Filet Mignon drizzled with a Merlot Sauce and topped with Wild Mushrooms are a tribute to Chef Patou. Sumptuous desserts offered are the succulent Lemon Bavarian Cream or the Swan of Dark Swiss Chocolate Mousse that are tempting endings to a classic French meal.

RECIPE SECRETS FROM MONSIEUR PATOU

Garlic Soup

Shrimp Salad Multicolor

Sole à la Basquaise

Citrus Cornish Hens

Chocolate Mousse

Garlic Soup

Serves 6
Preparation Time:
  1 Hour

  4 Tbsps. olive oil
  4 heads garlic, peeled
    and minced
  1 medium onion, sliced
  2 bay leaves
  2 sage leaves
    Sea salt and black
    pepper, freshly ground
  2 qts. chicken stock
  3 basil leaves, finely
    chopped
  6 egg yolks
  1 cup heavy cream
  1 cup croutons
  1 cup Swiss cheese,
    grated

Heat the olive oil in a medium pot over high heat. Stir in the garlic.

Add the onion, bay leaves, sage, salt and pepper and cook until the onion is golden brown. Stir constantly and reduce the heat if needed.

Add the chicken stock and basil. Bring to a boil and simmer for 45 minutes.

Remove the bay and sage leaves.

Beat the egg yolks in a large bowl and pour into the soup beating constantly. Add the cream and stir well.

Pour the soup into 6 warmed soup bowls. Top with croutons and sprinkle with grated cheese. Serve immediately.

Cooking Secret: If you need to reheat the soup, be sure to heat slowly over medium heat, stirring constantly, and serve immediately. Because of the addition of eggs, the soup cannot be boiled.

☆

Shrimp Salad Multicolor

Bring the stock to a boil over high heat. Add the shrimp and cook just until they change color.

With a sharp knife, cut tomatoes into ¼-inch cubes and set aside.

Divide the lemon juice between 2 small bowls. Chop apples and avocados into ¼-inch cubes. Place apple cubes in one bowl of lemon juice, avocado cubes in the other, and toss to prevent discoloring. Drain and set aside.

Place 1 Tbsp. each of the tomato, apple and avocado in a small bowl. Drizzle with peanut oil and toss to coat evenly. Set aside.

Coat the bottoms of 4 salad plates with vinaigrette. Add the shrimp to the remaining vinaigrette and toss to coat evenly. Transfer the shrimp to a strainer to drain excess dressing.

Arrange a ring of 18 shrimp on each plate, placing them tightly side by side. In the center of each shrimp ring, place one-fourth of the fruit mixture. Place the remaining cubed fruits outside the ring, alternating apple, avocado and tomato. Sprinkle the chives or scallions over the mixture in the center. Finally, garnish every other shrimp with a parsley leaf.

Cooking Secret: Chef Patou often prepares the vegetables in small balls. Lobster may be substituted for the shrimp.

Serves 4
Preparation Time:
 30 Minutes

- 2 cups fish stock
- 72 medium shrimp, raw
- 2 large tomatoes, cored, peeled and seeded
- 6 Tbsps. lemon juice
- 2 Granny Smith apples
- 2 medium avocados
- 1 Tbsp. peanut oil
- 1 cup vinaigrette
- 2 Tbsps. chives or scallions, minced
  Parsley for garnish

Sole à la Basquaise

Serves 6
Preparation Time:
  25 Minutes

- 2 **large red bell peppers**
- 2 **large green bell peppers**
- ⅓ **cup olive oil**
- 4 **large onions, peeled and sliced**
- 1 **small hot red pepper, sliced**
- 8 **garlic cloves, 4 chopped, 4 peeled**
- 2 **lbs. ripe tomatoes, peeled and chopped**
- 1 **bouquet garni (made with 1 leek leaf, bay leaf and parsley)**
  Sea salt and black pepper, freshly ground
- 6 **Dover sole, 8 to 10 oz. each**
- 1 **cup flour**
- ⅓ **cup olive oil**

O ver an open flame, grill the bell peppers to char and loosen their bitter skin. Remove the seeds and white pith. Under free-running water, wash the inside and remove the thin burned skin. Cut the flesh into wide strips.

In a large, heavy skillet, heat the olive oil and sauté the peppers over moderate heat. Cook for a few minutes, stirring regularly. Add the onions, hot pepper and 4 chopped garlic cloves. When tender, add the tomatoes and bouquet garni. Season with salt and pepper and cook over low heat for 10 minutes

Trim, gut and skin the sole. Cut the remaining 4 garlic cloves in half, then slice lengthwise into thin quarters and place on the fish. Season with salt and pepper and coat with flour.

In a large skillet, heat the oil and fry the sole over high heat for 4 minutes on each side. Reduce heat and add the hot vegetables. Cover and cook for 2 more minutes. Serve hot.

Cooking Secret: Traditionally, this fish is served whole but, you can fillet the sole and place them on a platter surrounded by the vegetables. Tuna can also be substituted for the sole.

Citrus Cornish Hens

Rinse the hens inside and out and pat them dry with paper towels.

Grate the zest from 3 of the grapefruits, leaving the bitter white pith. In a small bowl, pour boiling water over the grated zest and let it stand for 1 minute. Drain well.

In a small bowl, combine the grapefruit zest with butter and blend well. Spread 1½ Tbsps. of the grapefruit mixture under the breast skin of each hen.

Using a sharp knife, peel and section all the grapefruits, cutting between the membranes. Squeeze the membranes over a bowl and set aside ½ cup of the grapefruit juice.

Stuff the cavities of the hens with ½ of the grapefruit sections. Reserve the remaining sections for garnish.

Truss the hens and place in a medium roasting pan. Baste the hens with the reserved grapefruit juice and bake for 1 hour, basting every 15 minutes. The hens are done when the juice runs clear when a thigh is pricked. Transfer the hens to a warmed platter and cover loosely with aluminum foil.

Remove any fat from the juice in the roasting pan. Set the pan over moderate heat, add the port and bring to a boil. Reduce to a simmer and cook, stirring until the sauce is thickened. Strain the sauce and season with salt and pepper to taste.

Remove the trussing strings from the hens. Halve each bird lengthwise and discard the grapefruit sections. Arrange the hens on a serving platter. Garnish with the reserved grapefruit sections and sprinkle with pistachios. Serve with the sauce.

Serves 6
Preparation Time:
1½ Hours
Preheat oven to 375°

 6 **Cornish hens**
 6 **large grapefruits**
 ¼ **lb. unsalted butter**
 ½ **cup port**
    Sea salt and black
    pepper, freshly ground
 ⅓ **cup pistachios or**
    pecans

★

Chocolate Mousse

Serves 12
Preparation Time:
  30 Minutes
(note refrigeration time)

9 oz. semisweet dark
  chocolate
6 eggs
3 Tbsps. water
5 Tbsps. sugar
2 cups heavy cream
¼ cup Grand Marnier or
  Cointreau liqueur

reak the chocolate into small pieces and melt it slowly in the top of a double boiler over simmering water. When the chocolate is completely melted, set aside to cool.

In a metal bowl, separate the yolks from the egg whites. Set egg whites aside. Add the water and sugar to the yolks and whip vigorously over moderate heat until thick. Set aside.

In a second bowl, whip the cream until firm peaks form.

Mix the yolk mixture with the cool, melted chocolate. Add the whipped cream and set aside.

In a clean bowl, whip the egg whites until firm and shiny. Fold into the chocolate mixture. Transfer to individual mousse dishes if desired.

Refrigerate overnight.

Serve with liqueur drizzled over the top.

BOSCOBEL COTTAGE

185 Cordell Lane
Monroe, Louisiana 71202
(318) 325-1550
ROOM RATES: $75–$95

Boscobel Cottage, circa 1820, is one of the very few upland plantation cottages in existence and is entered in the National Register of Historic Places. Hewn timbers with mortise-and-tenon joinings were used in the foundation. Cypress and blue poplar were mainly used in the framing. Sassafras wood was used in the walls and ceiling of the drawing room and hall. The pine planks in the floors in all the rooms are 6 inches wide and 1¼ inches thick. The cottage stands proudly among champion pecan trees and lovely grounds, serving as a reminder of grander days gone by.

One of the favorite spots for relaxing or enjoying twilight cocktails is the garçonnière (bachelor's apartment) balcony, complete with swing and overlooking one of the New Orleans-style courtyards. Lacy wrought iron and lattice-dappled shade compliment yet another picturesque courtyard, which is a favorite site for breakfast. Here guests can see the squirrels and birds showing off their antics in century-old pecan trees.

Each guest room has its unique character and is located on the spacious grounds of the cottage. Air-conditioning, color TVs, VCRs, private baths, refrigerators, bottled spring water, refreshments to celebrate your arrival and a full Southern breakfast complete the fine "Louisiana-style" hospitality offered by your hosts.

Morning Glorious Muffins

Yield: 2 Dozen Muffins
Preparation Time:
  30 Minutes
Preheat oven to 375°

  2 cups flour
1¼ cups sugar
  2 tsps. baking soda
  2 tsps. ground cinnamon
½ tsp. salt
1½ cups carrot, shredded
1½ cups apple, peeled and
    shredded
¾ cup coconut
½ cup pecans, chopped
    and toasted
  3 eggs, beaten
  1 cup vegetable oil
½ tsp. vanilla

I n a large mixing bowl, combine the flour, sugar, soda, cinnamon and salt.

In a separate bowl, combine the carrots, apples, coconut and pecans. Stir in the beaten eggs, oil and vanilla. Add to the dry ingredients, stirring until moistened.

Grease muffin tins and spoon the prepared batter into them. Bake at 375° for 18 to 20 minutes.

Cooking Secret: These muffins freeze well.

FAIRFIELD PLACE

2221 Fairfield Avenue
Shreveport, Louisiana 71104
(318) 222-0048
ROOM RATES: $185–$250

Located in the beautiful Highland Historical Restoration District near Interstate 20, Fairfield Place welcomes visitors to the Shreveport-Bossier area with the legendary hospitality of the Deep South. Each spacious room features a private bath, king-sized beds, carefully selected antiques, color TVs and complimentary imported toiletries. The luxury suites have whirlpools and towel warmers. Works of art and books are in abundance throughout the inn, along with hand screened wall paper.

This beautifully restored Victorian mansion serves food to rival the best of the French Quarter. By combining an innovative menu with touches of elegance and a setting rich with the flavor of history, the hostess, Mrs. Lipscomb, treats her guests to daily culinary adventures.

You awaken to the smells of such delicacies as home-baked croissants with a spicy ham and cheese filling or a royal treat of Richard II Eggs. Add to that fresh fruit juice and plenty of steaming Cajun coffee or hot tea, served on fine china with heirloom sterling silver flatware, and you'll get an idea of hospitality in the style of Fairfield Place.

Marmalade Muffins

Yield: 8 Muffins
Preparation Time:
  45 Minutes
Preheat oven to 375°

  Oil for baking cups
  2 cups all-purpose flour
  ½ cup granulated sugar
  1 Tbsp. baking powder
  ¾ cup walnuts, chopped
  1 large egg
  1 cup plain yogurt or
    buttermilk
  ¼ cup butter, melted
  1 tsp. vanilla
  ½ cup orange marmalade

O il 8 muffin cups or use foil baking cups.
Thoroughly mix together the flour, sugar, baking powder and walnuts. Set aside.

In a medium bowl, whisk the egg with the yogurt, butter and vanilla until smooth. Pour this over the flour mixture, combining just until the dry ingredients are moistened.

Spoon 1 heaping Tbsp. of batter into each muffin cup. Press the back of the spoon into the batter to make a well. Fill the well with about 1 tsp. of the marmalade. Top with approximately 2 more Tbsps. of batter, or enough to cover marmalade.

Bake 25 to 30 minutes or until golden brown. Let cool about 5 minutes before removing from pan.

☆

Twenty-Four Thirty-Nine Fairfield

2439 Fairfield Avenue
Shreveport, Louisiana 71104
(318) 424-2424
ROOM RATES: $75–$125

At Twenty-Four Thirty-Nine Fairfield, you will experience the charm of Victorian elegance. The carved oak staircase invites you to explore the many collections of special interest, while the crystal chandeliers, the Victorian swag drapes of lace and moiré and the period antiques remind you of a gentler era.

Each room is different—some offer four-poster beds, a view of the private gardens, an antique brass bed with a feather mattress or a private whirlpool bath. Down pillows, handmade Amish quilts and down comforters will invite you to curl up and enjoy the cable television which is tastefully tucked away in the armoire.

The spicy aroma of gourmet breads, hot out of the oven, is part of the "proper" English breakfast that guests will savor. Fresh fruit, cheeses, homemade muffins, cereals, juice and coffee are followed by eggs, ham, sausage, fresh sautéed mushrooms and English muffins with homemade bread and butter. A luscious cup of hot tea from the kettle is the "proper" English way to end a delightful breakfast and begin a delightful day.

Green Bean Bundles

Serves 4
Preparation Time:
  45 Minutes
Preheat oven to 450°

64 fresh green beans
 3 Tbsps. brown sugar
 2 dashes allspice
 4 slices bacon

 team the green beans. Reserve about 1 cup of the bean water. Put the sugar and all spice in the water to dissolve and set aside.

Stretch a slice of bacon and cut in half. Place 8 of the steamed beans on the bacon and roll up tightly. Place in a lightly oiled baking dish. Continue until all the beans have been used.

Pour the water mixture over the beans and place in a 450° oven. Bake for 20 minutes, then turn the bundles over and bake for another 20 minutes until bacon is lightly browned.

★

Ham-Asparagus Rolls

Serves 6
Preparation Time:
  30 Minutes
Preheat oven to 400°

 2 bunches fresh
   asparagus spears
12 pieces of ham, thinly
   sliced
 2 Tbsps. butter or
   margarine
 2 Tbsps. flour
1½ cups milk
   Salt and pepper to
   taste
 1 cup sharp cheddar
   cheese, grated

team the asparagus until tender. Trim 1 inch from tip of each spear and reserve for garnish.

Roll several spears of asparagus in a slice of ham. Repeat until all have been used. Place in a shallow baking dish.

In a skillet, melt the butter. Add the flour and milk and season to taste, allowing the sauce to thicken. Add the cheese (reserve a small about of cheese for the top) and heat until melted. Pour over the ham rolls and top with reserved cheese.

Bake in a 400° oven until the sauce begins to bubble and the cheese is lightly browned.

To serve, place two ham rolls on each plate and drizzle with sauce. Garnish with reserved asparagus tips.

★

Tomato Quiche

Slice the onion very thin. Set aside.

Slice the tomatoes and arrange on the bottom of the pie crust. Sprinkle with the salt, pepper and basil and a layer of onions. Sprinkle the cheeses and cover the top entirely with the salad dressing.

Place in the oven and bake for 30 to 45 minutes at 400° until the top is lightly browned.

Let cool about 15 minutes before slicing. Garnish with a sprig of fresh basil.

Yield: a 10-inch pie
Preparation Time:
  1 Hour
Preheat oven to 400°

1 large onion
2 large tomatoes
1 pie crust, cooked to a
  very light brown
  Salt and pepper to
  taste
1 tsp. sweet basil
1 cup Monterey jack
  cheese, grated
1 cup sharp cheddar
  cheese, grated
1 cup Miracle Whip
  Fresh basil sprigs for
  garnish

Crossroads

Contact:

Louisiana Travel Promotion Association
P.O. Box 3988
Baton Rouge, Louisiana 70821
(504) 346-1857

Request information on these
  Crossroads subregions:
Natchitoches-Winnfield Area
Many-Leesville-DeRidder Area
Alexandria Area

I t has been said that the road to Louisiana's soul always leads to its heart, and Crossroads is that heart. It is the oldest permanent settlement in the Louisiana Purchase Territory, since 1714, and very proud of its heritage. Central Louisiana offers you a generous slice of colonial riches. From landmark plantations and historic towns to Creole and Cajun heritage, you'll experience the cultures that have made the state world famous. Romantic and historic bed and breakfasts, unique African-American history, natural splendors and antiquing all await you.

The unique architecture, including the largest assortment of Creole architecture in the Mississippi Valley, scenic beauty and the 33-mile-long Cane River Lake meandering beside historical landmarks and plantations, capture the imagination of its historic past.

Add to this the KISATCHIE NATIONAL FOREST, which offers picnic areas, fishing, hunting, canoeing and camping, with nature and hiking trails to enjoy the beautiful natural settings. Or get away to the "Garden In the Forest," HODGES GARDENS, for an interesting visit to the largest privately operated gardens in the United States. More than 4,700 acres include a multi-level seasonal 60-acre formal garden, old fashion rose garden, hiking and nature trails, picnic and historic area wildlife preserve and a 225-acre fishing lake.

Wild game is abundant in THREE RIVERS and RED RIVER STATE WILDLIFE MANAGEMENT AREAS, and in the BAYOU COCODRIE NATIONAL REFUGE. Nearby in **TUNICA-BILOXI,** more than 20,000 acres of lakes, bayous and rivers also provide abundant fish and game. If you prefer to view the animal kingdom in a more formal setting, the ALEXANDRIA ZOO is home to over 500 animals, including 20 endangered species in natural settings.

*Cotton is piled high on the lower
deck of a Mississippi riverboat.*

*A timber train loads logs
for the trip to the mill.*

Photos from the Louisiana Department of State,
Division of Archives, Records Management and History

FLEUR DI LIS BED AND BREAKFAST

336 Second Street
Natchitoches, Louisiana 71457
(800) 489-6621
(318) 352-6621
ROOM RATES: $60–$100

F leur di Lis, named after the royal symbol of France, is a charming Queen Ann Victorian house built in 1903. The bed and breakfast home offers spacious surroundings tastefully decorated with antiques and Victorian accents. In addition to beautiful woodwork such as massive cypress doors and ornamental molding, the inn has a grand, old-fashioned, wraparound porch, complete with rockers and a swing.

Five guest rooms, each with a private bath and a king- or queen-sized bed, are available. A full breakfast is served at their 12-foot-long Louisiana cypress table. Some of the favorite recipes of guests are goodies such as French Toast, Sausage Breakfast Casserole and Louisiana Breakfast Casserole.

Located in the Historic District, the inn is within walking distance of shops, restaurants, Northwestern State University of Louisiana and plantations along River Road.

French Toast

Spray or oil a 13×9-inch baking dish with Pam or any vegetable sprayCut bread into 1-inch slices and arrange in one layer in the dish.

In a mixing bowl, combine the milk, eggs, sugar, salt, vanilla, melted butter and nutmeg. Pour over the bread. Cover and refrigerate overnight.

Next morning, uncover and bake at 350° for 45 minutes or until puffy and browned.

Let stand for 5 minutes. Serve with warmed, flavored syrups or honey butter.

Serves 6 to 8
Preparation Time:
   45 Minutes
(note refrigeration time)
Preheat oven to 350°

   1 loaf French bread
   3 cups milk
   8 eggs
   4 tsps. sugar
   ¾ tsp. salt
1½ Tbsps. vanilla
   3 Tbsps. butter, melted
   ¼ tsp. nutmeg

JEFFERSON HOUSE

229 Jefferson Street
Natchitoches, Louisiana 71457
(318) 352-3957
ROOM RATES: $60–$110

You probably can't spell it or pronounce it, but you might remember Natchitoches from Steel Magnolias, the movie that put this small town on the map. But this spot in the center of the state had a special place in the heart of Louisiana long before the stars arrived. It is home to the famous Natchitoches meat pie, popular since before the Civil War. You can enjoy this traditional delight during the Christmas Festival of Lights at the Jefferson House, where your hostess hand prepares 300 pies each season.

Located on the beautiful Cane River in the historic district, within walking distance of local attractions, the Jefferson House offers accommodations in a quiet, comfortable and relaxed setting. Each room is tastefully decorated with antique and traditional furnishings, along with king-sized-beds.

Your hosts serve a full plantation-style breakfast each morning and offer cocktails each afternoon.

Natchitoches Meat Pie

Combine the beef and pork in a heavy skillet, browning over medium heat. Stir the meat until it crumbles. Remove from the skillet, drain and set aside.

Sauté the onion, pepper, green onions and garlic in the same skillet until tender. Return the meat to the skillet, stir in the flour and seasonings and set aside.

Make the pastry and divide into 4 portions. Roll out 1 portion to ⅛-inch thickness. Cut 5 circles, using a 6-inch saucer as a guide. Spoon about ¼ cup of the meat mixture on one half of the dough circle. Moisten edges with water. Fold the dough over the meat mixture, pressing edges to seal. Crimp edges. Repeat the procedure with remaining dough portions and meat mixture. Pies may be frozen before cooking.

Pour oil to a depth of 3 inches into a Dutch oven. Heat oil to 375°. Fry 4 pies at a time until browned, turning once. Drain on paper towels. Serve immediately.

Pastry

Combine the flour, baking powder and salt in a large bowl. Cut in the shortening with a pastry blender until the mixture resembles coarse meal. In a separate bowl combine the eggs and milk. Gradually add the milk mixture to the flour mixture, stirring with a fork until the dry ingredients are moistened. Shape into a ball (pastry will be stiff).

Yield: 20 Pies
Preparation Time:
  45 Minutes
Preheat oven to 375°

  1 lb. lean ground beef
  1 lb. lean ground pork
  1 medium onion,
    chopped
  1 medium green pepper,
    chopped
  1 bunch green onions,
    chopped
  4 to 5 cloves garlic,
    minced
  1 Tbsp. flour
  1 tsp. salt
  ½ tsp. pepper
  ¼ to ½ tsp. red pepper
    Pastry (recipe follows)
    Vegetable oil

Pastry:
  8 cups all-purpose flour
  2 tsps. baking powder
  4 tsps. salt
  1 cup shortening
  2 eggs, beaten
2¼ cups milk

★

THE LEVY-EAST HOUSE

358 Jefferson Street
Natchitoches, Louisiana 71457
(800) 840-0662
(318) 352-0662
ROOM RATES: $85–$150

The Levy-East House is nestled along the Cane River Lake in the quaint, historic town of Natchitoches, the oldest settlement in the Louisiana Purchase. The two-story Greek Revival house, circa 1838, was originally a one-story red brick structure with an upper story of wood added before the Civil War. The second-story balcony is graced with iron lace, offering guests the opportunity to absorb all the beauty and magic of this splendid historic area.

The four guest rooms are individually decorated with period antiques and precious heirlooms. Each room offers a luxurious queen-sized bed, television, telephone and private whirlpool bath. Central air conditioning assures your comfort, even on the warmest Southern night. A delicious Southern gourmet breakfast is elegantly served in the dining room.

Tastefully renovated to capture the spirit of an earlier time, the Levy-East House welcomes guests through its picturesque doors, in the tradition of Southern hospitality.

Creole Baked Eggs

Using a 6-cup muffin tin, place 1 tsp. butter in each muffin cup. Gently break egg into each cup and sprinkle with cheese, bacon and parsley. Add Creole seasoning, Worcestershire sauce and paprika to taste.

Bake at 350° for 15 to 20 minutes or until eggs are done to desired consistency.

Cooking Secret: Serve with cheese grits, strawberry bread, sausage and fresh fruit for a delicious Southern breakfast.

Serves 6
Preparation Time:
  30 Minutes
Preheat oven to 350°

  6 tsps. butter
  6 eggs
  6 tsps. cheese, grated
  6 tsps. bacon, crumbled
  6 tsps. parsley, minced
    Creole seasoning to
    taste (recommend
    Tony Chachere's)
    Worcestershire sauce
    Paprika

Loyd Hall Plantation

292 Loyd Bridge Road
Cheneyville, Louisiana 71325
(800) 240-8135
(318) 776-5641
ROOM RATES: $95–$125

S ituated on the banks of Bayou Boeuf, Loyd Hall Plantation's colorful past is marked by countless tales of survival throughout its 175-year history. This 640-acre plantation, in continuous operation since 1800, provides guests with a hands-on look at Louisiana agriculture, with crops of corn, cotton, soybeans and cattle. A few personal friends, like Clarence the donkey, will steal your heart. And the mysterious spirit of a violin player who appears at midnight on the second-floor verandah is one you'll always remember.

Loyd Hall features ornate plaster ceilings, suspended staircases and rare antiques. Charming and private bed and breakfast accommodations are truly one-of-a-kind.

Hot Artichoke Dip

Mix all ingredients thoroughly with mixer except the artichoke hearts. Fold in the artichokes.

Pour into pumpernickel loaf. Cover and bake for 1 hour at 350° or until heated thoroughly.

Serve hot with crackers, assorted breads or chips.

Serves 6 to 8
Preparation Time:
30 Minutes
Preheat oven to 350°

1 stick butter
1 cup sour cream
1 cup black olives, sliced
8 oz. cream cheese
1½ cups cheddar cheese, grated
1 cup green onions, chopped
White pepper to taste
Tabasco to taste
Artichoke hearts, drained, rinsed, quartered
1 round or oval pumpernickel loaf, hollowed out

Cajun Country

Get out the accordion and the fiddle. Put on your dancing shoes and have a good time. Wherever you go throughout Southwest Louisiana, you'll participate in the lively culture of the Cajuns. Music is everywhere. Food is delicious and zesty. Celebration is in the air. And by all means, take a swamp tour.

You may want to begin your visit to Southwest Louisiana in **LAKE CHARLES,** a hub of festivals, casinos and the CREOLE NATURE TRAIL, a national scenic byway. For the festival-minded, the ALLIGATOR HARVEST FESTIVAL is held in September and the CAJUN RIVIERA FESTIVAL in August attracts more than 13,000 people. A drive along the scenic byway offers the opportunity to view alligators, gulf beaches, birds and native wildlife.

Throughout Cajun Country, you'll find authentic Cajun and Creole cuisine, original Zydeco and Cajun music, scenic swamplands and many activities and sights characteristic of Louisiana's cultural uniqueness. Hunting and fishing or crabbing, shelling and bird-watching on miles of accessible beaches will entice visitors of all ages. Marsh flowers and marsh animals are prevalent in all the refuges and along the roads of this beautiful Acadian haven.

Contact:

Louisiana Travel Promotion Association
P.O. Box 3988
Baton Rouge, Louisiana 70821
(504) 346-1857

Request information on these
   Cajun Country subregions:
Lake Charles Area
Lafayette Area
New Iberia-Morgan City Area
Houma-Thibodauz-Grand Isle Area

Blessing of the fleet of shrimp boats.

LAFAYETTE in Cajun Country is also the heart of French Louisiana, offering museums, galleries and historical tours showcasing carefully crafted period homes filled with artifacts and antiques reflecting historic Acadian/Creole life.

A visit to **AVERY ISLAND,** home of Tabasco® brand pepper sauce, also offers the Jungle Gardens and Bird Sanctuary. Enormous flocks of egrets and herons, among other species, are protected here and may be seen in early spring and summer, while ducks and other wild fowl call Avery Island home in winter.

A cypress shack.

Photos from the Louisiana Department of State, Division of Archives, Records Management and History

A Louisiana bayou scene.

CAFÉ MILANO

ITALIAN with a hint of Creole
314 Belanger Street
Houma, Louisiana 70360
(504) 879-2426
Dinner Daily 11:30 a.m.–10:00 p.m.
AVERAGE DINNER FOR TWO: $50

Houma's newly launched Italian bistro, Café Milano, has already received superior restaurant reviews. Its warm and inviting atmosphere, friendly dining room staff and the wizards in the kitchen turn out some of the best Italian cuisine with a Creole flavor served anywhere.

Starters include fresh Tuna Salsa in a Grilled Creole Tomato or Frog Legs in a Spicy Fresh Orange Sauce. Pasta specials include the Penne in a Fresh Tomato, Basil and Kettle One Vodka Cream Sauce or the Rigatoni laced with Fresh Tomato, Artichokes, Diced Chicken Breast and Basil. Entrées range from Apple Crusted Veal Chops in a Port Wine Sauce to Rolled Fillet of Ruby Red Trout, Stuffed with Crawfish. The desserts are homemade and include Tiramisù, a variety of Cheesecakes or Zabaglione with Wild Berries.

RECIPE SECRETS FROM CAFÉ MILANO

Marinated White Bean and Shrimp Salad

Black Bean Soup

Mushroom Pasta with Tomato, Bacon and Cream

Tea Smoked Quail with Blackberry Sauce

Poached Apricots in Honey Vanilla Sauce

Marinated White Bean and Shrimp Salad

Soak beans overnight in cold water. Drain and remove any dirt or rocks. Cover with cold water, bring to a simmer and cook for 45 minutes or until tender. Drain and place in a bowl. Add the olive oil, 1 tsp. salt, pepper, parsley and garlic. Mix well. Let marinate in refrigerator for at least 1 hour.

Place remaining salt and shrimp into a medium-sized pot of boiling water and boil for 3 minutes or until tender. Drain shrimp.

Take the garlic cloves out of the beans and put in the shrimp. Add the juice of 2 lemons and mix gently until well blended.

On each of 4 individual serving plates, place 1 whole radicchio leaf, like a bowl. Divide the bean mixture into 4 portions and fill each radicchio bowl.

Garnish with slices from the remaining half lemon.

Serves 4
Preparation Time:
  15 Minutes
(note soaking and
  marinating time)

½ cup white beans, dry
1 cup olive oil, extra virgin
3 tsps. salt
1 tsp. black pepper, freshly ground
¼ cup fresh parsley leaves
4 cloves garlic, peeled
¾ lb. medium shrimp, peeled
2½ lemons
4 large radicchio leaves

Black Bean Soup

Yield: 1 gallon
Preparation Time:
2 Hours
(note soaking time)

1 lb. black beans, dry
¼ cup olive oil
1 large yellow onion,
   finely diced
2 stalks celery, finely
   diced
3 cloves garlic, minced
¼ cup flour
5 qts. vegetable stock
   Salt to taste
   Bouquet garni (made
   of 2 bay leaves, 1 tsp.
   cumin and 1 tsp.
   coriander)
   Black pepper, freshly
   ground, to taste
½ Tbsp. thyme, de-
   stemmed
1 Tbsp. oregano, freshly
   chopped
   Cilantro, for garnish

Soak the beans overnight. Drain, removing any dirt or rocks.

In a large stock pot put the olive oil, onion, celery and garlic, cooking until soft. Stir in the flour and cook for 2 minutes. Add the vegetable stock and bring to a boil. Add the beans and return mixture to a boil. Add salt and the bouquet garni and simmer uncovered for 2 hours or until beans are soft. Add more stock if necessary.

Remove the bouquet garni and purée half the beans. Return the puréed beans to the pot mixing with the other beans. Season with salt and black pepper to taste. Add the thyme and oregano.

Garnish with fresh cilantro before serving.

Mushroom Pasta with Tomato, Bacon and Cream

Bring a large pot of water to a boil for the pasta. Boil the pasta in boiling water for 4 minutes. Drain and set aside.

Sauté the pancetta and garlic in olive oil until pancetta is browned. Add the tomatoes, salt and pepper to the pancetta and cook until the tomatoes start softening. Add the stock and boil the mixture until it reduces by half. Add the basil, drained pasta and cream and toss together well. Cook 1 more minute, tossing occasionally.

Divide into 4 serving portions. Garnish with cheese and whole basil leaves.

* Pappardelle is a wide pasta noodle, about ⅝-inch thick, with rippled sides.

Cooking Secret: Fresh fettuccine can be used if pappardelle is not available.

Serves 4
Preparation Time:
  20 Minutes

1¼ lbs. fresh pappardelle*
  pasta, mushroom-
  flavored preferred
4 oz. pancetta (Italian
  bacon)
1 clove fresh garlic,
  minced
2 Tbsps. extra virgin
  olive oil
10 fresh Roma tomatoes,
  diced
  Salt and freshly
  ground black pepper
  to taste
1 cup vegetable stock
¼ cup fresh basil, torn
  into small pieces
  (reserve some whole
  for garnish)
½ cup heavy cream,
  room temperature
2 Tbsps. Parmesan,
  freshly grated

☆

Tea-Smoked Quail with Blackberry Sauce

Serves 4
Preparation Time:
  45 Minutes
(note refrigeration time)

  4 whole quail
  1/3 lb. coarse salt
     Cayenne pepper to
     taste
  1 cup sugar
  4 to 6 Tbsps. Earl Grey
     tea
     Blackberry Sauce
     (recipe follows)

Blackberry Sauce:
  2 to 3 lbs. fresh
     blackberries
  2 Tbsps. sugar
  1 cup water

R inse the quail in cold water and truss the legs tightly with twine. Fold the wing tips under the breast. Season well with salt and pepper and set in a glass bowl. Cover and refrigerate for 24 hours. Remove and wash well with cold water. Be sure to wash the cavity very well.

To smoke, line a roasting pan with aluminum foil. Sprinkle foil with sugar, tea and pepper. Set a rack inside the pan with the quail on top, taking care not to crowd them. Cover tightly and set on the stovetop at high heat for 15 to 20 minutes. Remove from heat and cool for 15 minutes.

Remove quail, being careful not to break the skin. Skin should be a nice mahogany color. Serve with Blackberry Sauce.

Blackberry Sauce
Push berries first through a strainer using a wooden spoon. Take the purée, if you desire to remove all seeds, and strain through a chinois*. Add the juice to a saucepan with sugar and water and simmer to the desired consistency.

* Chinois: A metal conical sieve with an extremely fine mesh, used for puréeing or straining. The mesh is so fine that a spoon or pestle must be used to press the food through it.

☆

Poached Apricots in Honey Vanilla Sauce

n a saucepan, slowly simmer together the water, honey, sugar and vanilla bean until all the flavors are well combined.

Add the apricots and poach approximately 2 minutes. The apricots should be tender, yet firm. Remove the apricots and reduce the sauce by half.

Place the apricots and sauce in glass and chill for 30 minutes. Garnish with fresh mint.

Serves 4
Preparation Time:
  35 Minutes

2 cups water
4 Tbsps. honey
4 Tbsps. sugar
1 vanilla bean, halved
   lengthwise
1 lb. fresh apricots,
   halved and pitted
   Fresh mint for garnish

CAFÉ VERMILIONVILLE

CAJUN
1304 West Pinhook Road
Lafayette, Louisiana 70503
(318) 237-0100
Open Daily 11 a.m.–10 p.m.
Saturday 5:30 p.m.–10 p.m.
AVERAGE DINNER FOR TWO: $90

L ong before the Civil War, experienced travelers knew that a stop at Vermilionville meant a warm "bienvenue" or warm welcome. Located in a restored landmark Louisiana structure, resting near the banks of Bayou Vermilion, Café Vermilionville still promises an exquisite meal served in a charming atmosphere 200 years in the making. The restaurant sits majestically on four acres, only minutes from any corner of this capital of French Acadiana.

A meal at Café Vermilionville is a unique combination of fine foods, ranging from entrées such as Bronzed Tilapia Fillet—laced with Grilled Onions, Peppers and Mushrooms, or Osso Bucco Milanese Braised Veal Shanks in a Spicy Herb and Vegetable Veal Demi-Glace, served on Angel Hair Pasta.

Under the direction of Chef/Owner Ken Vernon, the Café's place in culinary lore has long been secured by an impressive list of awards for creative excellence.

RECIPE SECRETS FROM CAFÉ VERMILIONVILLE

Fried Alligator with Dijon Mustard Sauce

Crawfish Beignets

Kahlua Grilled Shrimp on Angel Hair Pasta

Fried Alligator with Dijon Mustard Sauce

repare the sauce by combining the mayonnaise, mustard, salt and Tiger and Tabasco Sauces in a mixing bowl. Mix well.

Pound the alligator tenderloin fillets and marinate in the Dijon Mustard Sauce for 2 to 4 hours.

Coat the tenderloins with flour, then Dijon Mustard Sauce (reserve ½ cup) and then the bread crumbs. Fry at 350° until the meat is cooked through and lightly browned.

Serve hot with the remaining Dijon Mustard Sauce laced over the fillets.

Serves 4
Preparation Time:
  15 Minutes
(note marinating time)

  8 cups mayonnaise
  1 cup Dijon mustard
  ½ tsp. seasoned salt
  1 Tbsp. Tiger Sauce
  1 Tbsp. Tabasco Sauce
  5 lbs. alligator
     tenderloin, cut into
     four fillets
     Flour for coating
     Bread crumbs for
     coating
     Oil for frying

Crawfish Beignets

Yield: 50 Beignets
Preparation Time:
  30 Minutes

  2 lbs. crawfish tails,
    chopped
  2 cups Bacon Mirepoix
    (recipe follows)
  2 cups pepper cheese,
    shredded
  2 cups cheddar or
    Monterey Jack cheese,
    shredded
  2 cups buttermilk
  6 eggs
  1 tsp. seasoned salt
    Oil or butter for frying

Bacon Mirepoix:
  ¼ lb. bacon
  1 onion, chopped
  1 red bell pepper, diced
  1 gold bell pepper, diced
  1 green bell pepper,
    diced
    Seasoned salt to taste
  2 Tbsps. Tabasco Sauce

 n a large mixing bowl combine all the ingredients except the oil or butter. Form into triangles, (approximately 2 oz. each) and fry until golden.

Bacon Mirepoix:
Sauté the bacon until crisp, then add the onions and peppers and continue sautéing until vegetables are translucent. Add seasonings and adjust to taste.

Cooking Secret: The mixture freezes well prior to frying.

☆

Kahlua Grilled Shrimp on Angel Hair Pasta

Prepare the marinade by combining the Kahlua, honey, oil, Tiger Sauce, salt, garlic, parsley, Tabasco Sauce, basil, thyme and cilantro in a large mixing bowl. Marinate the shrimp for several hours.

Grill the shrimp and tomato over a charcoal fire with mesquite and hickory wood.

Reduce the veal stock and thicken with cornstarch. Add the Worcestershire sauce and red pepper.

Add the cooked pasta to the reduced veal stock.

Serve the shrimp over the pasta and garnish with the cilantro and grilled tomato.

Serves 6
Preparation Time:
  15 Minutes
(note marinating time)

- 2 cups Kahlua
- 2 cups honey
- 1½ cups salad oil
- 1¼ cups Tiger Sauce
- 2 Tbsps. seasoned salt
- 2 Tbsps. garlic, chopped
- 2 Tbsps. parsley, chopped
- 4 Tbsps. Tabasco Sauce
- 2 Tbsps. basil, chopped
- 2 Tbsps. thyme, chopped
- 2 Tbsps. cilantro, chopped
- 4 lbs. shrimp, peeled (10 to 15 count)
- 1 large tomato, quartered
- 4 cups veal stock
  Cornstarch to thicken
- 2 Tbsps. Worcestershire sauce
- 3 Tbsps. red pepper, chopped
- 1 lb. angel hair pasta, cooked
  Cilantro for garnish

☆

PREJEAN'S

NOUVEAU CAJUN CUISINE
3480 Highway 167 North
Carencro, Louisiana 70507
(318) 896-3247
Lunch and Dinner Daily 11 a.m.–11 p.m.
AVERAGE DINNER FOR TWO: $35

Upon entering Prejean's Restaurant you notice a glass display case filled with more than 120 state and national culinary medals, many of them gold medals. Executive Chef James Graham is widely recognized as one of the best Cajun chefs in the country—the irony being that he is originally from Montana and taught himself how to prepare Cajun dishes while working in Florida.

Graham describes his approach to cooking as "Infusion Cuisine," a blend of the best elements of Louisiana Creole, French and Cajun cooking. It taps into a growing trend in American cooking, he says. "As Americans have developed a taste for the deep and complex flavors of wine, they've looked to marry those wines with foods that have equally deep and intense flavors, like the rich and spicy sauces of South Louisiana."

RECIPE SECRETS FROM PREJEAN'S

Trio of Wild Mushrooms and Smoked Duckling Soup

Crawfish Étouffée

Crescent City Quail

Trio of Wild Mushrooms and Smoked Duckling Soup

Brown the duck bones in a 350° oven. Add the butter, leeks, carrots, parsnips, onion and garlic cloves. Stir well and continue to cook for 25 minutes, stirring often. Add the water and chicken stock and transfer the pan to the stove's top burner. Bring to a boil and cook at a low boil for 15 minutes. Strain the stock, discarding the leeks, onion and bones.

Reserve the carrots and parsnips. Dice them fine and set aside.

Bring the stock to a boil. Add a pinch of black and white pepper, cayenne pepper, thyme and bay leaf.

In a pan, melt the butter and sauté the mushrooms, cooking for 3 minutes. Add the flour and cook for 2 minutes.

Add the mushrooms to the boiling stock and stir until the roux dissolves from the mushrooms. Add the cooked duck, the reserved parsnips and carrots and the cream.

Serves 6
Preparation Time:
  1 Hour
Preheat oven to 350°

  3 hickory smoked
      cooked ducklings,
      deboned, reserving
      bones for stock
½ lb. butter
  2 leeks
  2 carrots
  2 parsnips
  1 onion
  3 garlic cloves
  3 qts. water
  1 qt. rich chicken stock
      Black and white
      pepper to taste
¼ tsp. cayenne pepper
¼ tsp. fresh thyme
  1 bay leaf
  4 Tbsps. butter
¾ cup whole morels
¾ cup whole chanterelles
½ cup shiitakes, sliced
  3 Tbsps. flour
¼ cup heavy cream

☆

Crawfish Étouffée

Serves 6
Preparation Time:
  30 Minutes

  3 sticks butter
  ⅓ cup flour
  2 small onions, finely
    diced
  ⅓ cup celery, finely diced
  ⅔ cup bell pepper, finely
    diced
  ¼ cup green onion
    bottoms
  2 Tbsps. paprika
  1 tsp. cayenne pepper
  1 tsp. black pepper
  ¾ tsp. garlic
  3 Tbsps. chicken
    bouillon
  2 lbs. crawfish tails
  2 Tbsps. parsley,
    chopped
  ½ cup green onion tops

ombine 1 stick butter and flour in a small saucepan. Stir while cooking for 3 minutes over medium-high heat to make a roux.

In a 4-quart saucepan, melt 1 stick butter and all onions, celery, bell pepper, green onion bottoms, spices, garlic and chicken bouillon. Cook for 2 more minutes while stirring. Add 1 qt. water and bring to a boil, boiling for 5 minutes.

Add the roux, stirring well with a wire whip. Reduce heat to medium and boil another 3 minutes.

Add the crawfish tails, onion tops and parsley. Add the last stick of butter and turn heat to low until ready to serve.

Note: This recipe won the 1994 World Étouffée Championship.

Crescent City Quail

Combine ingredients in a large mixing bowl and marinate quail for 1 hour.

For the mousse: In the food processor, purée the Cornish hen breasts. Place in a cold bowl with ice underneath it.

Purée the onions and add to the bowl. Add the mushrooms, chopped rosemary, chicken base, heavy whipping cream, garlic powder and cayenne pepper. With an electric mixer or by hand, whip all ingredients until cream sets, or about 4 to 5 minutes. Remove bowl to table.

With a rubber spatula, fold in the egg whites. Place the mousse in a pastry bag for stuffing the quail.

Remove the quail from the marinade and fill each quail's breast cavity with 4 Tbsps. of the wild mushroom and Cornish hen mousse.

Grill the stuffed quail, marking both sides with grill marks. Transfer to a baking sheet and finish in the oven at 350° for 8 to 10 minutes.

Slice each quail breast into 2 medallions, placing the body in the center of the plate, fanning medallions out.

Serves 6
Preparation Time:
  1 Hour
(note marinating time)
Preheat oven to 350°

Marinade:
  1 tsp. all-purpose Cajun
    seasoning
  1 Tbsp. Worcestershire
    sauce
  ¼ cup Bordeaux wine
  1 tsp. garlic, minced
  12 semi-boneless quail

Mousse:
  16 oz. Cornish hen breasts
  ¼ cup onion
  ½ cup morels, sliced
  2 tsps. fresh rosemary
    needles, chopped
  2 tsps. chicken base
  ½ cup heavy whipping
    cream
  ¼ tsp. garlic powder
  ¼ tsp. cayenne pepper
  2 egg whites, beaten to
    soft peaks and set
    aside in the
    refrigerator

☆

PRUDHOMME'S CAJUN CAFÉ

CAJUN CUISINE
4676 N. E. Evangeline Throughway
Carencro, Louisiana
(318) 869-7964
Lunch and Dinner Monday–Saturday 11 a.m.–10 p.m.
AVERAGE DINNER FOR TWO: $45

E nola Prudhomme and her family serve up authentic Cajun cuisine that's been associated with Louisiana and the Prudhomme name throughout the world for years. If you want the genuine food, this is the place—housed in a building constructed in the late 1800s.

Chef Prudhomme understands Cajun cuisine from the ground up, thanks to her family heritage. Along with her 11 sisters and brothers (including celebrity Chef Paul), she published "Prudhomme's Family Cookbook" and has won countless awards and medals for her menus.

Specialties include wonderful sautéed, fried and blackened Cajun dishes, pastas, steaks, low-fat entrees, homemade jalapeño bread, muffins, salads and desserts. Some of the highlights are her award-winning Catfish Enola, Pan-Fried Stuffed Catfish with Shrimp and Tasso Cream Sauce, Stuffed Red Snapper, Eggplant Rounds with Tasso Gravy and Pecan Cake.

RECIPE SECRETS FROM PRUDHOMME'S CAJUN CAFÉ'S

Broccoli Soup

Shrimp Pasta

Dutch Apple Cake

Broccoli Soup

In a large pot, bring water to a boil over high heat. Add the broccoli and continue to boil for about 20 minutes. Remove from heat and reserve 1 cup of the water; discard remaining water.

Place drained broccoli in a food processor and pulse until chopped. Do not over-process.

In a large pot over high heat, bring the whipping cream, canned milk and reserved cup of water to a boil. Reduce the heat to medium. Add the broccoli, salt and pepper; cook and stir for 15 minutes.

Melt butter in a medium skillet over medium heat. Add the flour. Cook and stir constantly until the flour turns the color of caramel. Remove from heat and slowly add to the broccoli mixture until soup is the desired thickness.

Serves 4
Preparation Time:
  45 Minutes

  8 cups water
  8 cups fresh broccoli
   florets
1½ qts. heavy whipping
   cream
  3 cups canned
   evaporated milk
2½ tsps. salt
  ⅛ tsp. ground red pepper
  ¼ cup unsalted butter
  ½ cup all-purpose flour

Shrimp Pasta

Serves 4
Preparation Time:
  30 Minutes

  1 lb. rotini pasta
  ¼ cup butter or
     margarine
  1 lb. medium shrimp,
     peeled, deveined
  2 tsps. seafood seasoning
  ⅓ cup shrimp stock or
     water
  ½ cup chopped green
     onion tops
  ¾ cup fresh mushrooms,
     sliced thin
  1 pint heavy whipping
     cream

Cook the pasta according to package directions; set aside.

     Over high heat, melt the butter in a 5-quart pot. Add the shrimp and 1 tsp. of the seasoning; cook and stir 2 minutes. Stir in the stock, or water and cook 7 minutes. Add the onion tops, mushrooms, remaining seasoning and whipping cream. Cook over medium heat for 6 to 8 minutes. Add the pasta to the shrimp and reduce heat to low. Cook for 3 more minutes.

☆

Dutch Apple Cake

Arrange the apple slices in a greased 9-inch square baking pan. Sprinkle the apples with brown sugar and pour 4 Tbsps. melted butter over the apple mixture.

In a medium bowl combine the flour, baking powder, salt and sugar. Stir well to mix.

In a separate bowl, blend together the egg, milk, vanilla, the remaining melted butter and the apple spice. Slowly add to the flour mixture. With a hand mixer on high speed, beat for 30 seconds or until the mixture is nice and fluffy. Pour the batter over the sliced apples and bake at 375° for 40 to 50 minutes. After removing from the oven, immediately loosen the cake from the sides of the pan. Turn upside down on a cake plate or board before serving.

Serves 8
Preparation Time:
 1 Hour
Preheat oven to 375°

 2 **cups sliced cooking**
   apples
 ½ **cup dark brown sugar**
 ½ **cup melted butter**
 1¼ **cups all-purpose flour**
 1¼ **tsps. baking powder**
 ¼ **tsp. salt**
 ¾ **cup granulated sugar**
 1 **egg, beaten**
 ½ **cup milk**
 ½ **tsp. vanilla extract**
 1 **tsp. apple spice**

☆

SPORTSMAN'S PARADISE

CAJUN
6830 Highway 56
Chauvin, Louisiana 70344
(504) 594-2414
Daily 5 a.m.–9 p.m.
AVERAGE DINNER FOR TWO: $40

Where to go for fresh fish? Sportsman's Paradise, of course, which is famous for its excellent variety of fresh seafood platters and the best gumbo in the state of Louisiana.

Menu highlights include the Sportsman's Super Platter, which includes Fried Fish, Shrimp, Oysters and Soft Shell Crab. A must try is the superb Bronzed Catfish and Fried Oysters. The secret ingredient in the delicious food at the Sportsman's Paradise is the chef and owner, Connie Scheer. She cooks fresh seafood deliciously, using a minimal amount of oil, highlighted with a touch of seasonings and spice. Her dessert specialty, Bread Pudding in Amaretto Sauce, is by itself worth a visit to her restaurant alone.

The decor is simple and comfortable and the service is excellent. Sportsman's Paradise is the perfect place for a family celebration or simply a great meal.

RECIPE SECRETS FROM SPORTSMAN'S PARADISE

Crab Meat Bundles

Cajun Shrimp and Corn Soup

Southern Fried Eggplant

Crab Meat Bundles

I n a large mixing bowl, combine the cream cheese and butter together. Add the garlic salt and onion powder. Mix well. Stir in crab meat and crab boil.

Cut the egg roll wrappers into quarters. Place 1 heaping tsp. of the crab mixture in the middle of each wrapper. Bring points of wrapper to center, moisten and pinch closed.

Fry at 350° until golden brown. Serve hot.

Serves 4
Preparation Time:
  20 Minutes

  3 **packages cream
    cheese, 8 oz. each,
    softened**
 ½ **stick margarine or
    butter, softened**
  2 **tsps. garlic salt**
  2 **tsps. onion powder**
  1 **lb. crab meat**
  1 **tsp. liquid crab boil**
  1 **package egg roll
    wrappers
    Oil for frying**

☆

Cajun Shrimp and Corn Soup

Serves 8
Preparation Time:
  20 Minutes

  1 **stick butter**
  1 **onion**
  3 **cloves fresh garlic,**
    minced
  2 **cans cream-style corn**
  1 **can stewed tomatoes,**
    diced
  2 **lbs. small shrimp,**
    peeled
1½ **pts. half and half**
1½ **pts. whipping cream**
  1 **lb. Velveta cheese**
    Salt and freshly
    ground black pepper,
    to taste
    Chives for garnish

Heat the butter in a large pot and sauté the onion and garlic until the onion is translucent.

Add the corn, tomatoes and shrimp and boil for 10 minutes. Reduce heat to medium and add the half and half, whipping cream, cheese, salt and pepper. When cheese melts, remove from heat.

Serve soup hot and garnish with freshly chopped chives.

Southern Fried Eggplant

Peel and slice eggplant into ¼-inch slices. Cover slices with 7-Up and soak for 3 hours.

Heat oil in a heavy frying pan. Dip eggplant in corn meal and fry until golden brown.

Cooking Secret: The 7-Up removes the bitter flavor sometimes associated with eggplant.

Serves 4
Preparation Time:
  15 Minutes
(note soaking time)

  2 **medium eggplants**
  1 **liter 7-Up**
     Oil for frying
     Corn meal for dipping

☆

INN AT LE ROSIER

314 East Main Street
New Iberia, Louisiana 70560
(318) 367-5306
ROOM RATES: $95

The Inn stands on oak-lined Main Street, once part of the estate that belonged to Shadows on the Teche, an ante bellum plantation built across the street on the banks of Bayou Teche. On the outside, le Rosier is a rather unpretentious but pleasing little white cottage standing behind a wrought-iron fence. Behind the gate, you'll find an elegant, highly acclaimed restaurant, serving up-scale Cajun fare. Some of the many specialties include Pan-Roasted Tilapia with Spinach, Shoestring Potatoes and Tarragon Beurre Blanc and Grilled Marinated Duck Breast with Wild Rice Tasso Dressing, Sautéed Mushrooms and Sweet Potato Hay.

If you continue along the scented garden path lined with gardenias, camellias, antique roses and magnolia trees, you will discover a traditional Acadian-style raised carriage house with four inviting guest rooms. The rooms are more modern in style than is found at many bed-and-breakfasts, offering king-sized beds, huge private bathrooms with ample storage space, television sets with full cable capacity and private telephones.

A sumptuous dinner, a comfortable night's lodging, a country breakfast—there is no more pleasant way to experience Acadiana and its prairies, moss-draped trees and Cajun heritage than a visit to le Rosier.

Crawfish in Spicy Creole Mustard

I n a large mixing bowl, combine the mustard, olive oil, vinegar, lemon juice, Worcestershire sauce, garlic, ketchup, Tabasco Sauce, paprika, lemon zest, 1 Tbsp. parsley, 1 Tbsp. green onion and pepper. Whisk until the rémoulade is well incorporated. This will taste better if made 24 hours in advance, then whisked again before use.

To roast peppers, place on barbecue grill, gas charbroiler or over an open flame on a gas stove burner. Do not try this with an electric stove top. Let the skin of the peppers char and blister on all sides. Place peppers in a bowl and cover with plastic food wrap. That allows the residual steam to loosen the skin from the pepper. Allow to cool, then peel peppers under cool, running tap water. Julienne and reserve in refrigerator.

To serve, toss the crawfish tails in rémoulade to taste, along with 1 Tbsp. parsley and 2 Tbsps. green onion.

Serve crawfish on top of baby lettuce, surrounded by a nest of julienned celery root and peppers. Perfect as an appetizer or light entrée.

Serves 6
Preparation Time:
  30 Minutes
(note time for flavors to
  blend)

¼ cup Creole mustard
½ cup olive oil
¼ cup rice vinegar
1 Tbsp. lemon juice
2 Tbsps. Worcestershire
  sauce
1 tsp. garlic, finely
  chopped, or ½ tsp.
  garlic powder
1 Tbsp. ketchup
6 dashes Tabasco Sauce
½ tsp. paprika
  Lemon zest from
  ½ lemon, finely
  chopped
2 Tbsps. parsley,
  chopped
3 Tbsps. green onion,
  chopped
  Black pepper to taste
1 red bell pepper,
  roasted and julienned
1 yellow bell pepper,
  roasted and julienned
1 lb. crawfish tails,
  rinsed
½ lb. baby lettuce
¾ cup celery root,
  julienned

Pecan Rice Pilaf

Serves 8
Preparation Time:
15 Minutes
(note refrigeration time)

6 cups wild pecan rice
(recommend Konriko
Brand)
¼ cup red onion, finely
chopped
1 cup roasted pecans,
chopped
½ cup green onion,
chopped
½ cup parsley, chopped
¾ red or green bell
pepper, chopped
2 Tbsps. jalapeño
pepper, finely chopped
¾ tsp. black pepper,
cracked
½ tsp. garlic powder
½ cup chicken broth
1½ cups fresh orange
segments or canned
mandarin orange
segments
½ cup raisins

C ook rice according to package directions.
Combine all other ingredients in large bowl, add
the cooked rice and mix until thoroughly incorporated.
Refrigerate and allow the flavors to blend. Wonderful as
a Cajun side dish.

☆

Louisiana Gulf Coast Crab Cakes

In a large mixing bowl, combine all the vegetables, herbs, salt, pepper, Tabasco Sauce, and lemon juice. Add 1 egg yolk, cream and 1½ cups bread crumbs.

Carefully fold in the crab meat, taking care not to break lumps up too much. Continue until well blended and able to be formed into patties.

Form 8 cakes by pressing mixture together with your hands so the cakes are packed tightly and will not break up.

Whisk remaining egg yolk with milk to form an egg wash. Dredge each cake thoroughly in the egg wash, then in flour and finally in the remaining ½ cup bread crumbs. Shake off excess bread crumbs.

Heat olive oil in a nonstick frying pan over high heat. Fry cakes until brown, for approximately 1 to 2 minutes per side, and drain on paper towels.

Place in a heated oven for about 2 minutes to heat through. Serve one cake per person with tartar sauce, salsa or aïoli.

Cooking Secret: Before dredging, if mixture is too dry and crumbling, add extra heavy cream; if too wet, add extra bread crumbs.

Serves 8
Preparation Time:
 30 Minutes

- 1 cup red bell pepper, finely chopped
- 1 cup green bell pepper, finely chopped
- 1 cup yellow bell pepper, finely chopped
- ¼ cup red onion, finely chopped
- ½ tsp. jalapeño pepper, finely chopped
- 1 cup tarragon
- 1 cup fresh basil
- 1 cup parsley
- 1 cup cilantro
- ¾ tsp. salt
- ¼ tsp. white pepper
- 1 dash Tabasco Sauce
- 1 tsp. lemon juice
- 2 egg yolks
- ½ cup heavy cream
- 2 cups bread crumbs
- 2 lbs. crab meat, picked through for shells
- 2 cups milk
- 1 cup flour
- 4 Tbsps. olive oil

☆

Roasted Tomato Soup with Tasso, Basil and Grilled Redfish

Serves 6
Preparation Time:
  30 Minutes

  1 lb. redfish or red
    snapper fillets
  1 Tbsp. olive oil
    Salt and pepper to
    taste
  1 tsp. garlic powder
  1 tsp. cayenne
  ½ cup + 1 Tbsp. flour
  8 Tbsps. (1 stick) butter
  2 medium yellow
    onions, chopped
  2 qts. chicken stock
  2 cups roasted or stewed
    tomatoes
  1 cup tasso, chopped
  2 cups Tabasco Bloody
    Mary Mix
  ½ tsp. coriander, ground
  3 Tbsps. dry basil
  ⅓ cup heavy whipping
    cream
    Tabasco Sauce to taste
  1 Tbsp. dry sherry
    Fresh basil for garnish

P repare the fish fillets by oiling them with olive oil. Lightly sprinkle with salt, pepper, garlic powder and cayenne pepper. Grill fish on gas charbroiler or outdoor pit on both sides until nicely marked, approximately 2 minutes. Remove from grill and set aside. After cooling, break the fillets up into bite-sized chunks and set aside.

Make the roux by mixing the flour and butter together over moderate heat and bring it to a bubble for 3 to 4 minutes. The roux should be watched and stirred so it does not brown and remains the color of butter. Add the onions and sauté for 4 to 5 minutes. While stirring, slowly add all the stock to the blond roux and bring to a simmer for 10 minutes.

Into the roux, add the tomatoes, tasso, bloody mary mix, coriander and basil. Allow to simmer 5 minutes. Add the grilled fish, heavy cream, Tabasco Sauce and sherry and return to simmer for 2 to 3 minutes. Adjust seasonings to taste with salt, pepper and Tabasco Sauce.

Serve garnished with fresh basil.

Cooking Secret: Shrimp may be substituted for redfish by placing 6 to 8 shrimp on a bamboo skewer. Oil and season with salt, pepper, garlic and cayenne. Grill for approximately 2 to 3 minutes per side. To serve, place shrimp in individual serving bowls and ladle soup over hot shrimp.

Tequila Key Lime Pie

Combine the lime juice, zest, tequila, egg yolks and sugar in a large stainless steel bowl. Incorporate well. Stir mixture in the top of a double boiler with a whip until thickened. Add the chopped butter, stirring well.

Pour into prepared pie shell. Refrigerate until center is firm and well set.

Yield: 1 pie
Preparation Time:
 30 Minutes
(note refrigeration time)

 ¾ cup lime juice
   Zest of 1 lime
 3 oz. tequila
   (recommend Cuervo
   Gold)
 10 egg yolks
 1 cup sugar
 8 Tbsps. (1 stick) butter,
   chopped
 1 prepared pie shell

☆

LA MAISON DE CAMPAGNE

"The Country House"
825 Kidder Road
Carencro, Louisiana 70520
(318) 896-6529
ROOM RATES: $95–$110

O nce the family home for the owners of a large, prosperous sugar cane and cotton plantation, The Country House has been restored to its original grand style of country Victorian elegance. Located in the heart of Acadiana, among live oak and pecan trees, its site is a serene country setting, fifteen minutes north of downtown Lafayette.

Each guest room has been meticulously decorated and furnished with antiques. Slumber on canopied beds or cuddle up under a handmade quilt in one of three guest rooms, all with private baths and walk-in closets.

In the morning, you'll be greeted by your hosts, Joeann and Fred, and ushered into the dining room where a full Cajun country gourmet breakfast is served. Joeann takes great pride in her culinary expertise, as she skillfully prepares scrumptious homemade breads, pastries and unique egg dishes. Her specialties include homemade sweet potato cake rolls and praline or strawberry sweet bread.

Pig's Ears
Les Oreilles de Cochon

I n a mixing bowl, combine the yeast, sugar and water. Stir until dissolved. Add the salt and flour, using your hands to mix until the dough is formed into a ball. Divide into 18 balls.

Spray your work surface and rolling pin with a non-stick spray. Roll each ball to ⅛-inch thickness, into a "pig's ear."

Drop into 2-inch-deep hot oil, holding the center down with a fork until the "ears" puff up. Drain. Drizzle each ear with cane syrup and sprinkle with pecans. Serve warm.

Yield: 18 Pig's Ears
Preparation Time:
  1 Hour

  1 tsp. yeast
  2 tsps. sugar
  1 cup warm water
  ½ tsp. salt
1½ cups all-purpose flour
    Oil for frying
    Cane syrup
    Pecans, chopped

☆

Sweet Potato Cake Roll

Serves 12
Preparation Time:
  30 Minutes
(note refrigeration time)
Preheat oven to 375°

Cake:
  3 eggs
  1 cup sugar
  ⅔ cup cooked, mashed
    sweet potatoes or
    yams
  1 Tbsp. lemon juice
  ¾ cup flour
  1 tsp. baking powder
  1 tsp. cinnamon
  ½ tsp. ground ginger
  ¼ tsp. nutmeg
  ½ tsp. salt
  ¼ cup pecans, chopped
    Powdered sugar

Filling:
  8 oz. cream cheese
  4 Tbsps. butter or
    margarine
  1 cup powdered sugar
  2 tsps. concentrated
    orange juice (or 1 tsp.
    orange juice
    concentrate and 1 tsp.
    lemon juice)
  ½ tsp. grated orange peel
    or dried orange zest

L ine a 10-inch × 15-inch jelly-roll pan with waxed paper. Grease and flour the paper.

Beat the eggs at high speed with a mixer for 5 minutes. Add the sugar gradually. Stir in the yams and lemon juice. Set aside.

In a separate bowl, combine the flour, baking powder, spices and salt. Fold into the yam mixture.

Pour the batter into the prepared jelly-roll pan. Sprinkle nuts on top and bake for 15 minutes at 375°. Turn cake out onto waxed paper sprinkled with powdered sugar.

Spread filling on the cake. Roll up cake with filling. (Recipe follows).

Chill for 2 to 4 hours before serving. Sprinkle with powdered sugar before serving.

Filling
In a mixing bowl combine the cream cheese and butter, whipping together until fluffy. Add the sugar and juice; beat until smooth. Add the grated orange peel or zest.

☆

Steamed Yeast Rolls

Warm the milk in a saucepan over low heat, then add the yeast and sugar. Remove from heat and allow to stand for 5 minutes.

Add ½ butter, bread flour, ¼ tsp. salt, eggs and vanilla extract. Knead on a floured board for 8 to 10 minutes (or use dough hook). Let rise 30 minutes in a covered bowl. Divide dough into 18 equal pieces and roll into balls.

Spray the bottom and sides of a covered skillet (9 inches at least) with a nonstick spray. Melt 1 tsp. or butter or margarine in bottom, coating evenly. Sprinkle bottom of pan evenly with ¼ tsp. additional salt. Place rolls in the pan on top of salt and butter cover, and allow to rise 30 minutes.

Pour water over the rolls, cover and place over low heat until you smell the rolls. Do not uncover during the process, but do watch carefully to avoid burning. This usually takes 7 to 10 minutes.

Place the rolls in a small pool of the Vanillin Sauce, (recipe follows) then drizzle remaining sauce over the top.

Vanillin Sauce:

Combine t6he egg yolks, sugar and milk in a heavy saucepan over low heat. Stir almost constantly over low to medium heat until the sauce is slightly thickened and begins to coat a wooden spoon. Do not boil or it will curdle. Add the vanilla.

Yield: 18 rolls
Preparation Time:
  1½ Hours
(note rising time)

  ½ cup whole milk
  1 pkg. yeast
  7 Tbsps. sugar
  ½ cup + 1 tsp. melted
    butter
  3 cups bread flour
  ½ tsp. salt
  2 eggs, beaten
  ½ tsp. vanilla extract
  ⅓ cup water

Vanillin Sauce:
  6 beaten egg yolks
  ½ cup sugar
2½ cups whole milk
  1 tsp. vanilla extract

Le Jardin Sur Le Bayou

256 Lower Country Drive
Bourg, Louisiana 70343
(504) 594-2722
ROOM RATES: $85, including a gourmet breakfast

Enjoy Cajun hospitality on this 26-acre registered wildlife sanctuary, featuring century-old live oaks and native plants teeming with hummingbirds and butterflies. Stroll quiet garden paths under an oak canopy, pause at bridges and enjoy goldfish ponds, a swing or just sitting on a garden bench and watching the extensive variety of birds.

A comfortable and tastefully decorated private upstairs suite, set back from a quiet country road, offers central air and heat, cable TV, telephone, refrigerator, use of screened breezeway and laundry facilities. Owners and innkeepers Dave and Jo Ann Cognet create magical breakfasts each morning, served in the garden or dining area overlooking the fish ponds.

This highly recommended bed and breakfast inn is just one hour from New Orleans. Consider staying at least two nights to enjoy the home cooking and garden tour.

Fresh Cherry Muffins

In a large mixing bowl, cream the butter, then add the sugar and beat until light and lemon colored. Beat in the eggs.

Sift together the dry ingredients and add to the butter mixture beginning and ending with 1 Tbsp. milk.

Stir in the cherry halves, pecans and almond extract.

Bake in paper-lined muffin tins in a 375° oven for 15 to 20 minutes. If making mini loaves, adjust the time accordingly, about 25 to 30 minutes.

Cooking Secret: This recipe, developed by Kathy Holt, is delicious right out of the oven. Make plenty—they also freeze well.

Yield: 12 to 16 large muffins or 4 mini loaves.
Preparation Time: 45 Minutes
Preheat oven to 375°

½ cup butter or margarine
1 cup sugar
2 eggs
2 cups all-purpose flour
½ tsp. salt
½ tsp. baking soda
1 Tbsp. double-acting baking powder
2 Tbsps. buttermilk or sour milk
1 cup fresh or frozen cherry halves (pitted)
¾ cup chopped pecans
2 tsps. almond extract

OLD CASTILLO BED AND BREAKFAST

P.O. Box 172
St. Martinville, Louisiana 70582
(318) 394-4010
ROOM RATES: $50–$80

Almost beneath the moss-draped branches of the legendary Evangeline Oak, the Greek revival structure of the Old Castillo Hotel rises from the banks of historic Bayou Teche. You are invited to step back in time, share in the warmth of Acadian culture and cuisine and cherish leisurely time spent beside the slow-moving Bayou waters.

The rooms are spacious, equipped with private baths, elegant antiques, queen-sized, four poster beds and dreamy Bayou views. Each morning you are treated to a deliciously prepared full Cajun breakfast.

Corn and Crab Bisque

Sauté the onions in butter over low heat. Add the flour and mix well. Let simmer for 5 minutes.

Add the two cans of corn, crab meat, milk, whipping cream, evaporated milk, chicken base, white pepper and Accent. Simmer for 15 minutes. Do not boil.

In a small bowl or cup combine the cornstarch and water and add to the soup. Simmer for 10 minutes more and add the parsley flakes, onion tops and stock or water.

Cook 5 minutes more. Serve hot.

Serves 6
Preparation Time:
   20 Minutes

   2 medium onions, finely
      chopped
   8 Tbsps. (1 stick) butter
   1 cup flour
   1 can whole kernel corn
   1 can cream-style corn
   1 lb. white crab meat
   1 qt. milk
   1 qt. heavy whipping
      cream
   2 cans evaporated milk
1½ Tbsps. chicken base
   ½ Tbsp. white pepper
   2 Tbsps. Accent

Cornstarch Roux:
   2 Tbsps. cornstarch
   ⅔ cup water
   ⅛ cup parsley flakes
   ⅛ cup green onion tops,
      chopped
   2 cups chicken stock or
      water

Ramsay-Curtis Mansion

626 Broad Street
Lake Charles, Louisiana 70601-4337
(318) 439-3859
ROOM RATES: $95–$225

Located in the heart of the Charpentier Historic District stands the Ramsay-Curtis Mansion. The huge, rambling Queen Anne Revival mansion shows the craftsmanship and the pride and joy the builder took in his work.

Intricate and charming details can be seen on the exterior with ornamental features such as the lovely "Juliet Balcony," or the side portico with arched supports made of limestone. The original carriage house remains at the rear of the property.

Gracious living describes the many interior features including elegant yet comfortable rooms with private baths, TVs, phones and fax service. Enjoy hand-carved banisters and stained glass windows separated by a terra cotta brick fireplace. Original light fixtures adorn the recessed library, along with paneled ceilings and a marble fireplace with a carved wooden mantle. Also, glass-front bookcases and cabinets line the walls, and the leaded, beveled window, which is imported from Italy shows the Ramsay family crest.

Sugar and Spice Pumpkin-Nut Bread

I n a large mixing bowl, combine the pumpkin, sugar, milk and eggs.

In a separate bowl sift together the flour, baking soda, baking powder, salt and spices. Add to the pumpkin mixture.

Add the butter and blend well. Stir in the nuts and bake in a well-greased standard loaf pan at 350° for 45 to 55 minutes.

Cooking Secret: This bread freezes well.

Yield: 1 loaf
Preparation Time:
 1 Hour
Preheat oven to 350°

 1 cup pumpkin purée
1¼ cups sugar
 ½ cup milk
 2 eggs
 2 cups flour
 ½ tsp. baking soda
 2 tsps. baking powder
1¼ tsps. salt
1½ tsps. cinnamon
 ¾ tsp. nutmeg
 1 tsp. pumpkin pie spice
 ¼ cup butter, softened
 1 cup pecans, chopped

Plantation Country

Contact:

Louisiana Travel Promotion Association
P.O. Box 3988
Baton Rouge, Louisiana 70821
(504) 346-1857

Request information on these
   Plantation Country
   Subregions:
Baton Rouge Area
Great River Road Area

Harvesting sugar cane.

*Photo from the Louisiana Department of State,
Division of Archives, Records Management
and History, John B. Gasquet Collection*

Here you see Louisiana's past, her present and her future. **BATON ROUGE,** the state capitol, sits at the heart of this remarkable region. It's the perfect location for exploring the great English plantations around **ST. FRANCISVILLE** and **JACKSON** and the magnificent Creole plantations near **NEW ROADS** and down the Great River Road.

Laced by swamps, bayous and lakes and bisected by the Mississippi River, Plantation Country is divided into two subregions, the Baton Rouge Area and the Great River Road Area.

You can see for miles along the Mississippi River from the top of the Capitol, travel back in time at one of the many historical sites such as MAGNOLIA MOUND, tour elegantly restored ante-bellum homes, embark upon a mysterious swamp tour, enjoy riverboat casinos and taste fine Cajun, Creole and Old South cuisine.

Ancient Acadian and Creole traditions still abound in Plantation Country's Great River Road Area. Drive by or visit plantation homes, centuries-old cemeteries and ferry boats moored along the Great River Road on both sides of the Mississippi River. It is the home of Andouille Sausage, Br'er Rabbit, the CATFISH and ALLIGATOR FESTIVALS and the PLANTATION PARADE, where visitors are invited to tour, eat, sleep and enjoy the cultural richness of Louisiana.

The State Capitol in Baton Rouge.

JOE'S "DREYFUS STORE" RESTAURANT

LOUISIANA CUISINE
Highway 77 South
Livonia, Louisiana
(504) 637-2625
Lunch Tuesday–Sunday 11 a.m.–2 p.m.
Dinner Tuesday–Saturday 5 p.m.–9 p.m.
AVERAGE DINNER FOR TWO: $50

I t's not the kind of place you just run across. Someone has to tell you about this restaurant. No fuss, just great flavor, offering traditional recipes for Shrimp Remoulade, Fried Oysters, Joe's Fried Fresh Fat Soft-Shell Crabs or the Catfish Breaux Bridge, a fried whole catfish on rice, swimming in crawfish étouffée.

Step through the door onto old wood floors, with farm implements and framed hodgepodge on the walls, to a big room of tables with plates mounded high with traditional Louisiana cuisine. This site has been the Dreyfus General Store since the 1890s. The restaurant run by Louisiana natives Joe and Diane Major draws rave reviews as well as crowds from miles around.

RECIPE SECRETS FROM JOE'S "DREYFUS STORE"

Marinated Crab Fingers

Corn and Shrimp Soup

Bread Pudding with Rum Sauce

Marinated Crab Fingers

n a mixing bowl combine the crab meat with the oils, lemon juice, vinegar, onion, celery, carrot and seasonings. Mix well and chill for 24 hours before serving.

Serves 6
Preparation Time:
 5 Minutes
(note marinating time)

5 lbs. crab fingers (crab meat)
1 cup vegetable oil
4 Tbsps. olive oil
¼ cup lemon juice
4 Tbsps. vinegar
1 onion, thinly sliced
1 stalk celery, thinly sliced
1 carrot, thinly sliced
Dash of Worcestershire sauce
Salt and pepper to taste
Red pepper to taste

☆

Corn and Shrimp Soup

Serves 6
Preparation Time:
  45 Minutes

  4 oz. salt pork belly,
    diced, optional
  1 large onion, diced
  1 large bell pepper, diced
  ½ stalk celery, diced
  1 stick butter
  2 Tbsps. flour
  2 qts. shrimp stock
  1 lb. fresh ripe tomatoes,
    peeled, seeded,
    chopped
    Salt and pepper to
    taste
  2 lbs. small shrimp,
    heads on, or 1 lb. small
    shrimp, peeled

Sauté the diced pork until lightly browned. Add the onion, bell pepper, celery and butter. Cook until the onion is translucent. Add the flour. Cook for 5 minutes, stirring.

Add the shrimp stock, corn, tomatoes and seasoning. Simmer for 25 minutes. Add the shrimp and simmer for 10 more minutes Season to taste before serving.

☆

Bread Pudding with Rum Sauce

I n a large bowl, combine the sugar, cinnamon, nutmeg, vanilla, eggs and egg yolks with a hand whip. Add the milk, raisins and coconut and stir until thoroughly combined.

Add the bread slices, gently pushing them down into the milk mixture. Do not squeeze. Let the slices soak for 30 minutes, turning occasionally.

In a small bowl, cream the butter and powdered sugar. Generously coat the sides and bottom of a 9 × 13 × 2-inch cake pan (preferably glass) with half the butter-sugar mixture. Reserve the other half.

Pour the pudding into the prepared pan. Pat down. Gently push raisins into the mixture so they will not burn in the oven.

Melt the remaining butter-sugar mixture. Pour on top of the pudding.

Place the pan on a cookie sheet and bake at 325° for 45 to 50 minutes in the top third of the oven. Allow pudding to cool before serving.

For the sauce: In a small saucepan, combine the butter, powdered sugar and cream. Bring to a boil over medium heat, stirring constantly. Remove from heat and add the rum. Cool and pour on top of pudding before serving.

Serves 6
Preparation Time:
  1¼ Hours
Preheat oven to 325°

  2 cups sugar
  ½ tsp. ground cinnamon
    Pinch of nutmeg
  1 tsp. vanilla
  4 eggs plus 2 egg yolks
  1 qt. whole milk
  ½ cup raisins
  1 cup sweet coconut,
    shredded
  1 loaf day-old French
    bread, cut into ½-inch
    slices
  4 Tbsps. soft unsalted
    butter
  4 Tbsps. powdered sugar

Rum Sauce:
  4 Tbsps. unsalted butter
  ½ cup powdered sugar
  ½ cup whipping cream
  1 Tbsp. Myer's dark rum

LAFITTE'S LANDING

FRENCH AND CAJUN CUISINE
10275 Highway 70 Access
St. James, Louisiana
(504) 473-1232
Lunch 11 a.m.–3 p.m.
Dinner 6 p.m.–10 p.m.
Sunday Brunch 11 a.m.–3 p.m.
AVERAGE DINNER FOR TWO: $55

Almost 200 years ago a legend was born. His name was Jean Lafitte. The name of this legend is about all that historians can agree on. There is disagreement about his birthplace, marriage (or marriages) and even the time and place of his death. But there is no disagreement that Jean Lafitte was the most colorful character in the entire history of Louisiana. He was denounced as a pirate, a scoundrel and a smuggler. He was admired as a corsair, a privateer and a gentleman rover. Poets signed for the man who committed "a thousand villainies and a single heroism."

Chef John Folse acquired the Old Viala Plantation home in 1978, when it was moved to its present site at the western approach to the Sunshine Bridge, and established his Lafitte's Landing Restaurant with his indigenous Louisiana cuisine. Menu highlights include a thick wedge of fresh Tuna that is Charbroiled and topped with Grilled Shrimp and Roasted Tomato Salsa on Tequila Lime Butter. The Fresh Salmon Fillets are rubbed with Citrus and Horseradish, then topped with Pan-Fried Scallops on Julienned Vegetables. A Roasted Herb-Encrusted Rack of Lamb is served with Caramelized Sweet Potatoes and Mayhaw Pepper Jelly Glacé and the 10-oz. Veal Chop is Pan-Roasted and served with a Wild Mushroom Flan and Roasted Shallot Glace. Absolutely delicious.

RECIPE SECRETS FROM LAFITTE'S LANDING

Louisiana Seafood Gumbo

Cajun Stuffed Rack of Lamb

Orange Cane Syrup Pecan Pie

Louisiana Seafood Gumbo

I n a 7-qt. cast-iron Dutch oven, heat the oil over medium-high heat. Sprinkle in the flour and using a wire whisk, stir constantly until a brown roux is achieved. Do not allow the roux to scorch. Should black specks appear in the roux, discard and begin again.

Once the roux is golden brown, add the onions, celery, bell pepper, garlic and sausage. Sauté for approximately 3 to 5 minutes. Stir the claw crab meat into the roux. This will begin to add the seafood flavor to the mixture. Slowly add hot shellfish stock, one ladle at a time, stirring constantly until all is incorporated.

Bring to a low boil, reduce to simmer and cook approximately 30 minutes. Add additional stock if necessary to retain volume.

Add green onions and parsley. Season to taste using salt, pepper and Louisiana Gold. Fold shrimp, lump crab meat, oysters and reserved oyster liquid into soup.

Return to a low boil and cook approximately 5 minutes. Adjust seasoning and serve over cooked rice.

Serves 6
Preparation Time:
  1 Hour

  1 **cup vegetable oil**
  1 **cup flour**
  2 **cups onions, chopped**
  1 **cup celery, chopped**
  1 **cup bell pepper,**
     chopped
  ¼ **cup garlic, diced**
  ½ **lb. Andouille sausage,**
     sliced
  1 **lb. claw crab meat**
  3 **qts. shellfish stock**
  2 **cups green onions,**
     sliced
  ½ **cup parsley, chopped**
     Salt and cayenne
     pepper to taste
     Louisiana Gold Pepper
     Sauce to taste, optional
  1 **lb. shrimp, peeled,**
     deveined
  1 **lb. jumbo lump crab**
     meat
  24 **oysters, shucked**
     (reserve liquid)
  6 **cups rice, cooked**

☆

Cajun Stuffed Rack of Lamb

Serves 6
Preparation Time:
  1 Hour

  6 lamb racks
  Salt and pepper to
  taste
  1 cup shrimp, cooked,
  chopped
  1 cup claw crab meat
  ¼ cup onions, finely
  diced
  ¼ cup green onions,
  finely diced
  1 Tbsp. garlic, diced
  1 Tbsp. red bell pepper,
  diced
  ½ cup béchamel sauce
  ½ cup seasoned Italian
  bread crumbs
  Salt and cayenne
  pepper to taste
  ¼ cup butter, melted
  2 Tbsps. dried thyme
  2 Tbsps. dried basil
  1 Tbsp. dried tarragon
  1 Tbsp. crushed
  rosemary
  2 Tbsps. garlic, diced
  Salt and cracked black
  pepper to taste
  1 cup red wine
  3 cups demi-glace

Using a 6-inch paring knife, cut a ¾-inch slit in the center of the lamb loin. Be sure not to cut completely through the meat. The pocket should be large enough to hold a generous portion of the stuffing. Lightly season the inside of the pocket with salt and pepper. Set aside.

In a large mixing bowl, combine the shrimp, crab, onions, garlic, bell pepper, béchamel sauce and bread crumbs, blending well to ensure that all seasonings are evenly mixed. Season to taste using salt and pepper. The stuffing should be moist but stiff enough to stand on its own. Add more bread crumbs or béchamel if necessary. Stuff each loin with an equal amount of the seafood stuffing. Set aside.

On a large baking pan with a 1-inch lip, place stuffed lamb racks. Moisten with melted butter and season generously with thyme, basil, tarragon, rosemary and garlic. Season to taste using salt and cracked black pepper.

Place the racks on the baking pan, bone side up and bake approximately 25 minutes for medium-rare. Remove from oven and deglaze the baking pan with red wine, making sure to scrape bottom well.

Pour these ingredients into a 10-inch sauté pan and add demi-glace. Bring to a boil and reduce until slightly thickened. Using a sharp knife, slice lamb racks into four chops each and top with a generous portion of demi-glace.

☆

Orange Cane Syrup Pecan Pie

I n a large mixing bowl, combine eggs and sugar. Using a wire whisk, whip until well-blended. Do not over-beat. Add the Karo and cane syrups, blending into the egg mixture. Add the orange juice, orange peel and flour. Blend until all is well incorporated. Add the chopped pecans and fold once or twice into the mixture. Pour mixture into pie shells.

Place the pecan halves in a circular pattern on the outer edges of the pie. Place pies on a cookie sheet covered with parchment paper.

Bake approximately 1 hour and check for doneness. It is best to cool the pies overnight before serving.

Yield: 2 pies
Preparation Time:
  1¼ Hours
Preheat oven to 350°

  10 **eggs**
   1 **cup sugar**
   2 **cups light Karo syrup**
   1 **Tbsp. cane syrup**
  ½ **cup freshly squeezed**
     orange juice
   1 **Tbsp. orange peel,**
     grated
   2 **Tbsps. flour**
  1½ **cups pecans, chopped**
   2 **unbaked 10-inch pie**
     shells
  16 **pecan halves**

MAISON LACOUR

FRENCH
11025 North Harrell's Ferry Road
Baton Rouge, Louisiana 70816
(504) 275-3755
Lunch Monday–Friday 11:30 a.m.–2 p.m.
Dinner Monday–Saturday 5:30 p.m.–10 p.m.
AVERAGE DINNER FOR TWO: $100

A cozy cottage nestled among live oaks and crape myrtles, together with a private collection of antiques, create a country home ambiance of warm elegance offering French Epicurean delights.

Only the highest-quality ingredients are used, offering a wide selection including veal, game, beef, fowl, lamb and seafood. The dinner menu offers classic dishes like the veal chops and wild boar or venison. Culinary creations like *John's Favorite,* which consists of a broiled tenderloin medallion with shrimp and lump crab in puff pastry with hollandaise. In a class by themselves are the crusty loaves of bread and signature desserts.

The wine list offers a wide selection of California and French vintages.

RECIPE SECRETS FROM MAISON LACOUR

Stuffed Mushrooms with Crawfish

Soup Jacqueline

Assorted Green Salad

Shrimp Baton Rouge

Sabayon Glacé

Stuffed Mushrooms with Crawfish

Melt 4 Tbsps. butter in a sauté pan. Add the celery, bell pepper, shallots and garlic. Sauté for 1 minute, being careful not to burn the garlic.

Add the tasso and crawfish meat. Lower the heat and cook for 5 minutes.

Add salt, cayenne and ¼ cup bread crumbs. Remove from heat and allow to cool to room temperature, about 30 minutes.

When mixture has cooled, mix in the egg yolks.

Clean the mushrooms and discard the stems. Brush the olive oil on the inside and outside of each mushroom cap. Arrange the caps in a shallow casserole dish. Stuff and mound each mushroom cap with the crawfish mixture, sprinkle with the remaining bread crumbs and drizzle with 2 Tbsps. of melted butter.

In preheated oven bake the stuffed mushrooms for 15 minutes or until brown. Serve immediately.

Serves 6
Preparation Time:
55 Minutes
Preheat oven to 375°

   6 **Tbsps. butter**
 ½ **stalk celery, finely chopped**
 ½ **bell pepper, finely chopped**
   4 **Tbsps. shallots, finely chopped**
   2 **cloves garlic, finely chopped**
   2 **oz. tasso or cured ham**
   1 **lb. crawfish tail meat, coarsely chopped**
 ½ **tsp. salt**
 ½ **tsp. cayenne pepper**
 ⅓ **cup dry bread crumbs**
   2 **egg yolks**
 24 **medium mushrooms**
   4 **Tbsps. olive oil**

Soup Jacqueline

Serves 6
Preparation Time:
  30 Minutes

- 2 Tbsps. shallots, finely chopped
- 2 Tbsps. chopped celery stalk
- 2 Tbsps. vegetable oil
- ⅓ cup flour
- 3½ cups clam juice
- ¼ tsp. white pepper
- 1 cup cream
- 3 oz. Brie, trimmed and cubed
- 8 asparagus stalks, blanched and diced
- 8 oz. lump crab meat

In a medium saucepan, sweat the shallots and celery in oil for about 1 minute.

Add the flour and mix well, but do not let it brown. Stir in the clam juice, stirring until smooth, and season with pepper. After the mixture thickens, add the cream and bring to a boil. Lower heat and simmer for 20 minutes.

Add the Brie and stir until the cheese is melted.

Add the diced asparagus and crab meat and cook for 3 minutes. Check seasoning.

Ladle into 6 heated soup bowls and serve immediately.

☆

Assorted Green Salad

Wash the greens well, removing any heavy stems, and dry thoroughly. Tear greens into bite-sized pieces and place in a salad bowl. Toss gently to mix the leaves.

Prepare the salad dressing by mixing the sugar, pepper, water, salt, cayenne and vinegar until salt and sugar are completely dissolved, then add the salad oil. Let stand for a few hours before serving.

Shake well and pour over greens just before serving.

Toss gently and divide among 6 salad plates.

Serves 6
Preparation Time:
  15 Minutes
(note standing time)

¼ **cup arugula**
½ **cup frisée or curly**
   chicory
½ **cup Boston lettuce**
½ **cup green leaf lettuce**
2 **Tbsps. sugar**
¼ **tsp. black pepper**
2½ **Tbsps. hot water**
1½ **tsps. salt**
⅛ **tsp. cayenne**
2 **Tbsps. red wine**
   vinegar
⅓ **cup light salad oil**

☆

Shrimp Baton Rouge

Serves 6
Preparation Time:
  30 Minutes

4 Tbsps. olive oil
1 lb. angel hair pasta
¼ lb. butter
⅓ cup salad oil
1 garlic clove, minced
1 shallot, minced
4 Tbsps. green onions,
  minced
2 cups heavy cream
  Juice of l lemon
1 tsp. black pepper,
  ground
½ tsp. cayenne
½ tsp. white pepper,
  ground
1 tsp. dry mustard
1 tsp. prepared
  horseradish
1 tsp. Worcestershire
  sauce
1 tsp. salt
4 Tbsps. Dijon mustard
30 shrimp, peeled and
  deveined

Bring 2 qts. of water to a boil. Add 1 Tbsp. olive oil. Separate strands of angel hair pasta and drop into boiling water. Cook for 2 minutes. Drain and rinse with hot water. Toss with 3 Tbsps. olive oil and keep warm until ready to serve.

In a large sauté pan, heat butter and salad oil until they foam. Add the garlic, shallot and onions. Cook for 1 minute, being careful not to burn the garlic.

Add the heavy cream, lemon juice, spices, horseradish, Worcestershire sauce and salt. Simmer for 10 minutes. Whisk in the Dijon mustard.

Add the shrimp and cook until they are plump, about 4 to 5 minutes.

Arrange shrimp on angel hair pasta and pour sauce over them.

Sabayon Glacé

our the wine and the raspberry liqueur into a saucepan, bring to a boil and lower heat, letting it simmer for 5 minutes.

Meanwhile combine the egg yolks, water, sugar and cornstarch in the bowl of a mixer and beat at medium-high speed until the mixture forms a ribbon.

Use the low speed of the mixer while pouring in the hot wine and liqueur mixture. Return the mixture to the saucepan and set over low heat, stirring continuously with a whisk until mixture thickens to whipped-cream consistency.

Remove the pan from the heat.

Pour this custard into a bowl. Place in the refrigerator to chill for about 3 hours, stirring from time to time to prevent a skin from forming. This dessert may be made 1 day ahead, covered and refrigerated.

To serve, combine the well-chilled cream with vanilla in a chilled mixing bowl and beat at medium speed for 1 or 2 minutes; then increase the speed and beat for another 3 to 4 minutes, until the cream begins to thicken. It should be a little firmer. Do not overbeat or the cream may turn into butter.

Still beating, incorporate the cold wine custard and beat for about 3 minutes, until the mixture is homogeneous and very light in texture, like a mousse.

Serve in 6 chilled dessert dishes. Garnish with raspberries or berries of choice and with a sprig of mint. Cover and refrigerate.

Cooking Secret: This dish can be prepared and refrigerated up to 3 hours in advance.

Serves 6
Preparation Time:
  30 Minutes
(note refrigeration time)

- 1½ cups medium dry white wine
- ½ cup raspberry liqueur
- 6 egg yolks
- 2 Tbsps. water
- ½ cup granulated sugar
- 1 Tbsp. cornstarch
- 2 cups heavy cream, well chilled
- 1 tsp. vanilla
- 1 pt. fresh raspberries, blackberries, strawberries or blueberries
- Mint for garnish

BARROW HOUSE INN

9779 Royal
St. Francisville, Louisiana 70775
(504) 635-4791
ROOM RATES: $95–$150

Situated on the banks of the Mississippi River, in the heart of plantation country, St. Francisville is the site of the Barrow House Inn. The inn is actually two guest houses, circa 1809 and the late 1700s. Both are listed on the National Register of Historic Places.

Rooms and suites are furnished in quality antiques such as full tester and canopy beds, armoires, rocking chairs and claw-footed bathtubs. One suite even features a mattress stuffed with Spanish moss, a material used for 125 years in Louisiana bedding. The inn is also home to 21 original Audubon prints (West Feliciana Parish was Audubon's beloved "happy-land"). Guests are invited to walk among the azaleas, camellias and huge live oaks; watch the goldfish swim in the pond or simply relax in a rocking chair on the front porch.

Chef and innkeeper Shirley Dittloff offers her widely acclaimed gourmet dinners by candlelight in the historic dining room. Guests are offered the choice of a continental or a full "Feliciana" breakfast. Both breakfast and dinner are served with formal settings of sterling silver and fine china, in an atmosphere of casual elegance.

Creole Eight-Bean Soup

C over beans with water 2 inches above them and soak overnight. Drain.

To the beans, add the onion, celery, bell pepper, ham hocks or salt pork, bay leaves, tomatoes with juice, seasonings, bouillon cubes and water. Bring to a boil, cover and simmer 1½ hours.

Add the ham and andouille sausage and simmer ½ hour. Add the okra or green beans and simmer an additional 15 minutes. Check seasonings and add salt and Tabasco Sauce to taste.

Serves 8
Preparation Time:
  2¼ Hours
(note soaking time)

  2 cups or 1 lb. mixed
     dried beans
  1 cup onion, chopped
  ½ cup celery, chopped
  ½ cup bell pepper,
     chopped
  2 ham hocks or 2 thick
     slices of salt pork
  3 bay leaves
  1 can of chopped
     tomatoes, 14 oz.
  1 tsp. thyme
  ½ tsp. oregano
  ¼ tsp. cayenne pepper
  ½ tsp. black pepper
  1 tsp. garlic powder
  2 beef bouillon cubes
 10 cups water
  1 cup ham, chopped
  1 cup andouille sausage,
     sliced
1½ cups sliced okra or
     green beans
     Salt and Tabasco Sauce
     to taste

Mexicajun Potato Pie

Serves 8
Preparation Time:
1 Hour
Preheat oven to 350°

1 pkg. frozen hash
   brown potatoes, 12 oz.,
   thawed
3 medium eggs, beaten
½ cup milk
¼ cup picante sauce
1 cup cheddar cheese,
   shredded
2 green onions, chopped
¼ cup cilantro or parsley,
   chopped
¼ tsp. salt
¼ lb. tasso, chopped

C ombine all the ingredients in a large mixing bowl. Pour into a greased 10-inch pie plate.

Bake at 350° for 50 minutes to 1 hour or until the mixture is set and golden brown. Remove from heat and let stand for 5 minutes. Slice into 8 pieces.

☆

Praline Parfait

Melt the butter in a large pot. Add the sugars and cream. Cook for 1 minute stirring constantly. Add the milk and half the pecans. Cook for 4 minutes, stirring occasionally.

Reduce heat to medium and continue cooking another 5 minutes. Add the remaining pecans and vanilla. Continue cooking for another 15 to 20 minutes.

Place 1 scoop of vanilla ice cream into a fluted glass. Drizzle the hot praline sauce on top. Garnish with whipped cream and pecans.

Serves 6
Preparation Time:
 30 Minutes

12 Tbsps. (1½ sticks)
 butter or margarine
 1 cup sugar
 2 cups packed light
 brown sugar
 ½ cup heavy cream
 1 cup milk
2½ cups chopped pecans
 1 tsp. vanilla
 1 qt. vanilla ice cream
 Whipped cream for
 garnish
 Chopped pecans for
 garnish

NOTTOWAY PLANTATION

Mississippi River Road
P.O. Box 160
White Castle, Louisiana 70788-0160
(504) 545-2730
ROOM RATES: $95–$250

At the edge of the cane fields, Nottoway stands overlooking the Mississippi. This enormous mansion, completed in 1859, reflects an unusual combination of Neo-Classical architectural elements blended with touches that were the fanciful desires of the original owner. Not only is the floor plan irregular, but the house contained many elements that were innovative and rare in the mid-19th century, such as indoor plumbing and hot and cold running water.

Today, overnight guests may stay in the original bedrooms in the main house, or in rooms in the "boys' wing," or the Overseer's Cottage. The Master Bedroom Suite is furnished with the antique marriage bed and other bedroom furniture that belonged to the original family.

Overnight guests and visitors receive a complimentary tour of the house, a glass of sherry upon arrival, an early morning wake-up call with hot coffee and sweet potato muffins, as well as a full breakfast. Chef Johnny "Jambalaya" Percle runs Randolph Hall, the restaurant on the grounds. Chef Percle is noted for his Cajun and Creole specialties, including his signature Bacon, Lettuce and Tomato Soup.

Sweet Potato Cinnamon Muffins

In a mixing bowl, blend together the mashed sweet potatoes with the melted butter. Add the milk and vanilla. Add the flour, baking powder, sugar, salt and cinnamon and stir to blend. Don't overmix.

Spoon dough into muffin tins lined with paper cups. Bake at 450° for 15 minutes.

Yield: 12 muffins
Preparation Time:
  25 Minutes
Preheat oven to 450°

  ¾ cup sweet potatoes,
    cooked and mashed
  ¼ cup butter, melted
  ⅔ cup milk
  ¼ tsp. vanilla
  1¼ cups flour
  4 tsps. baking powder
  2 Tbsps. sugar
  1 tsp. salt
  1 tsp. cinnamon

☆

OAK ALLEY PLANTATION

3645 Louisiana Highway 18
Vacherie, Louisiana 70090
1-800-44 ALLEY
(504) 265-2151
ROOM RATES: $95–$125

A visit to Oak Alley Plantation begins with its spectacular trees. A quarter-mile alley of twenty-eight sheltering oaks over 250 years old greets visitors today. The present-day plantation, a National Historic Landmark, was built in 1839, when Southern aristocracy ruled the land.

Bed-and-breakfast accommodations are available in four turn-of-the century Creole cottages (a total of five separate units) located in the residential section of the plantation, not far from the ante bellum mansion. Each cottage is individually furnished and cheerfully decorated with the fresh charm of country living. The three large cottages offer fully stocked kitchens and can accommodate up to 6 people each. The absence of television and telephones in all the cottages further enhances the peaceful, relaxing setting.

Guests enjoy a full country breakfast served at the plantation restaurant, which specializes in Cajun and Creole dishes.

Pecan Pralines

Combine the butter, milk and sugar in a saucepan. Add the vanilla extract. Cook over high heat to a rolling boil. Lower temperature to medium and continue to boil for 20 minutes, stirring constantly.

Remove from heat. Add the pecans and stir until the mixture thickens. Quickly drop onto greased foil. Let cool before serving.

Yield: 48 to 58 pieces
Preparation Time:
  30 Minutes

$\frac{1}{2}$ lb. butter
 3 cans evaporated milk
 8 cups granulated sugar
$\frac{1}{3}$ cup vanilla extract
 8 cups pecan pieces,
  shelled

ROSEDOWN PLANTATION

12501 Highway 10
St. Francisville, Louisiana 70775
(504) 635-3332
ROOM RATES: $95–$145

I n the golden years of the 19th century, the land along the lower reaches of the Mississippi River was home to huge plantations that lined the banks of the river, from Natchez to New Orleans. More than half of America's millionaires in the 1850s were living in this rich valley.

Nowhere was the opulence of the plantation society more apparent than at Rosedown Plantation. Built in 1835, it was owned by a wealthy cotton planter, Daniel Turnbull, and his wife Martha. Perfectionists with a rare artistic sense, Martha and Daniel filled the mansion with treasures from America's finest cabinetmakers, with elegant wall coverings, chandeliers, silver and marble statuary. Rosedown with its 28 acres of historic gardens is first and foremost a distinguished landmark for visitors to the South.

The overnight accommodations allow guests the opportunity to experience life in an American time capsule. Guests are invited to stroll the formal gardens, visit the historic outbuildings and enjoy a guided tour of Louisiana's most distinguished museum house. Rosedown offers 11 guest suites with private baths, antique furnishings with historical themes, canopied beds, a swimming pool, tennis courts and continental breakfast.

Pound Cake

I n a large mixing bowl beat together the butter, margarine and cream cheese. Add the sugar, mixing well. Add the vanilla, salt and eggs, one at a time, beating well after each addition. Slowly add the flour.

Pour the batter into a 10-inch tube or bundt pan. Place the pan in a cold oven. Bake at 275° for 1½ hours. Remove from oven and let cool in pan.

Cooking Secret: This treasured recipe is from Mrs. Turnbull's housewarming party representing 150 years of time-honored tradition and delicious dining.

Serves 6
Preparation Time:
   30 Minutes

   1 **cup (2 sticks) butter**
   ½ **cup (1 stick) margarine**
   8 **oz. cream cheese**
   3 **cups sugar**
   1 **Tbsp. vanilla**
      Dash salt
   6 **eggs**
   3 **cups cake flour**

Greater New Orleans

Contact:

**New Orleans
Metropolitan Convention
and Visitors Bureau**
1520 Sugar Bowl Drive
New Orleans, Louisiana 70112
(800) 672-6124
(504) 566-5005

**Louisiana Travel Promotion
Association**
P.O. Box 3988
Baton Rouge, Louisiana 70821
(504) 346-1857

*The Cabildo in New Orleans,
site of the signing of the
Louisiana Purchase in 1803.*

F rom the heart of New Orleans to elegant small towns on Lake Pontchartrain's north shore, you'll find nonstop history, festivals and natural beauty. Drive scenic byways, dine at outdoor cafés, enjoy fabulous shopping, visit world-class attractions or charter a boat and go deep-sea fishing in the Gulf of Mexico.

The Greater New Orleans Area is made up of two subregions, the North Shore Area and the New Orleans Area. Located on the north shore of Lake Pontchartrain, the natural environment offers fishing, boating, tubing, camping and golf as well as trails for bicycling, horseback riding, skating, walking or jogging. Located less than one hour from New Orleans, at the intersection of Interstate 55 and Interstate 12, you will find a 1,000-foot swamp walk, an alligator farm and a 900-acre exotic animal safari. You will also find an eclectic selection of restaurants, festivals and events reflecting the cultural diversity.

Jazz, outdoor cafés, fine restaurants, museums, the legendary FRENCH QUARTER and MARDI GRAS are some of the fascinating contrasts that entice the whole family to **NEW ORLEANS**. Its waterways offer riverboat cruises on the Mississippi or boating on Lake Pontchartrain. Experience the renowned zoo and aquarium, wax and art museums, shopping and the excitement of casino gaming or a marshland excursion. Mardi Gras alone brings two weeks of parades and balls in early spring. The Carnival season is followed by the

An artist in Jackson Square, New Orleans.

SPRING FIESTA, the JAZZ AND HERITAGE FESTIVAL, the FRENCH QUARTER FESTIVAL, LA FÈTE, BASTILLE DAY, NEW ORLEANS FOOD FESTIVAL and many more. The SUPERDOME holds major sporting events, including the SUPER BOWL. Every parish in this lively Louisiana region has year-round activities and acres of historical tours.

St. Louis Cathedral and Jackson Square in New Orleans. The inscription on the statue of Andrew Jackson reads, "The Union Must & Shall Be Preserved."

Photos from the Louisiana Department of State, Division of Archives, Records Management and History.
Photo of Jackson Square from the John B. Gasquet Collection.

ALEX PATOUT'S
LOUISIANA RESTAURANT

CAJUN
221 Royal Street
New Orleans, Louisiana 70130
(504) 525-7788
http://www.patout.com
Dinner daily beginning at 5:30 p.m.
AVERAGE DINNER FOR TWO: $70

C hef Alex Patout no longer views himself so insistently as the bearer of 165 years of family cooking tradition, seeing himself instead as a transition to the Louisiana cuisine of the future.

As chef, as restaurateur, as food purveyor and as media personality, Patout has matured in his grasp of the story line developing with the state's two bountiful styles, Creole and Cajun. And he has sensed the world maturing with him, from followers of a fad to devotees of a rich and varied menu.

"The basic trend," observes the chef-owner of Alex Patout's Louisiana Restaurant, "is taking the best local ingredients and the heritage of a cooking style that is absolutely country and adapting it with the help of ongoing modern techniques." His passion for Louisiana cooking has also produced a Cajun cookbook and a food line featuring entrées, meats and salad dressings. *Food and Wine* magazine has proclaimed him one of the top 25 chefs in America, while *Esquire* named him one of the "men under 40 who are changing America."

At Alex Patout's, the lighting is subdued, the service polished, the linen impeccable and down-home cookin' is raised to sophisticated heights. Cochon du Lait, for example, consists of a whole pig, roasted very slowly in a pit, then sliced and served with pork gravy, sweet potato praline casserole and spiced apple chutney. The roast rack of lamb is a four-rib rack, roasted in a slightly sweet Creole mustard sauce and served with a port wine demi-glace.

RECIPE SECRETS FROM ALEX PATOUT'S

Cajun Stuffed Mushrooms

Seafood Gumbo

Smothered Duck

Maque Choux

Pineapple Upside-Down Cake

Cajun Stuffed Mushrooms

R emove the stems from the mushrooms and reserve them for another use (a good Cajun never throws anything away). Wipe the caps

Sauté the onion, bell peppers and celery in ½ lb. of butter until soft. Stir in the crab meat and ½ cup lemon juice and simmer for 10 minutes.

Add the green onions, parsley and bread crumbs. Add a dash each of Worcestershire and Tabasco Sauce. Simmer 4 to 5 minutes, stirring often. Season with salt and pepper to taste. Remove dressing from heat and let cool.

Stuff the mushroom caps generously with the dressing and place in a single layer in a shallow ovenproof dish. Melt the remaining ½ pound butter and add the remaining 6 tablespoons of lemon juice and 2 tablespoons each of Worcestershire and Tabasco Sauce and the vermouth.

Simmer together for 1 minute, pour over the mushrooms and bake in a preheated 350° oven for 15 minutes, or broil at 450° for 5 minutes.

Serves 8 as a first course
Preparation Time:
  30 Minutes
Preheat oven to 450°

- 24 large, fresh mushrooms
- 2 medium onions, chopped fine
- 2 medium bell peppers, chopped fine
- 2 celery ribs, chopped fine
- 1 lb. butter
- 2 lbs. white crab meat
- ½ cup + 6 Tbsps. fresh lemon juice
- 4 Tbsps. green onions, chopped
- 4 Tbsps. parsley, chopped
- 2 cups plain bread crumbs
- 2 Tbsps. + a dash of Worcestershire sauce
- 2 Tbsps. + a dash of Tabasco Sauce
  Salt, black pepper, white pepper to taste
- 3 tsps. ground red pepper or to taste
- 4 Tbsps. dry vermouth

☆

Seafood Gumbo

Serves 6
Preparation Time:
  3 Hours

  2 Tbsps. salt
  2 tsps. ground red
    pepper
  2 tsps. ground black
    pepper
  1 tsp. ground white
    pepper
  1 lb. fresh okra, sliced
    ¼-inch thick
  ½ cup vegetable oil
  1 tsp. white vinegar
  2 cups water
  3 large tomatoes, peeled
    and roughly chopped
  4 medium onions,
    chopped fine
  6 fresh crabs (preferably
    blue)
  2 lbs. fresh medium
    shrimp with heads
  6 qts. water
  3 medium bell peppers,
    chopped fine
  1½ cups dark roux*
  1 cup green onions,
    chopped
  1 cup parsley, finely
    chopped
  6 cups rice, cooked

I n a small bowl, mix together the salt and peppers, set aside.

Place the okra, oil, vinegar, water, tomatoes, ¼ of the onions and 2 tsps. of the salt-pepper mixture in a large 8 to 10 qt. stock pot. over medium heat, stirring well. Cover and reduce heat, cooking the vegetables for 45 minutes to 1 hour, stirring often. If the mixture begins to stick, add a little water to dilute.

While the okra is cooking, half-fill a large stock pot with water and bring to a boil. Add the crabs, cover and cook for 4 minutes. Drain the crabs and cool.

Peel and devein the shrimp, and place the peels and heads in the empty stock pot. When the crabs have cooled enough to handle, detach the claws, crack both joints and add them to the stock pot. Remove the crab fingers and add 6 qts. of water, then boil for 1 hour. Strain the stock, then return it to the pot and place over medium heat. Discard the shrimp heads and peels, reserving the crab claws and fingers for the finished gumbo, if desired.

Add the remaining onions, bell peppers, the cooked okra, the remaining salt-pepper mixture and the roux. Stir well, bringing the mixture to a boil. Let simmer for 1 to 1½ hours. The gumbo should not be too thick, but run freely off a spoon. If it becomes too thick, add water.

Add the crab claws and fingers to the gumbo and continue to simmer over low heat for 45 minutes to 1 hour. If you are cooking your gumbo for the next day, remove from heat and let cool. Remove the crabs from the gumbo, pick out the meat and return the meat to the pot, discarding the shells.

Before serving, bring the gumbo to a slow simmer over medium heat. Add the shrimp and cook until they are pink and firm, 4 to 6 minutes. Stir in the green onions and parsley, remove from heat and serve in large soup bowls over beds of cooked rice.

* Roux is a mixture of flour and fat, such as butter or drippings from pork or beef fat, that is cooked to a deep golden brown.

☆

Smothered Duck

n a small bowl, mix together the salt and peppers. Season the ducks inside and out with about half the mixture.

Place the flour in a large flat pan and dredge the ducks lightly on all sides.

Place the oil in a Dutch oven or other large, heavy pot over medium-high heat and brown the ducks well on all sides. Remove the ducks to a platter and discard all but 1 Tbsp. of the oil. Add the onions, bell peppers and celery to the pan, reduce the heat to low, and sauté for 2 to 3 minutes.

Return the ducks to the pot, stir well and add the stock. Cover the pot and cook over low heat until the ducks are very tender, about 3½ to 4 hours. Stir occasionally to avoid sticking.

Remove the ducks from the heat and let stand a few minutes to allow the fat to rise to the top. Skim and discard the fat and stir in the green onions and parsley.

Cooking Secret: *Smothering* is a multipurpose Cajun technique that works wonders with everything from game to snap beans. It is similar to what the rest of the world knows as braising, where the ingredients are briefly browned or sautéed, then cooked with a little liquid over low heat for a long time. The result is a tender, satisfying dish that makes its own gravy. Other game and poultry that work well this way are squirrel, rabbit, hen and quail.

Serves 8
Preparation Time:
  4 Hours

  1 Tbsp. salt
  2 tsps. ground red
    pepper
  2 tsps. ground black
    pepper
  1 tsp. ground white
    pepper
  2 to 3 fresh ducks (4 to
    5 lbs. each)
1½ cups all-purpose flour
 ½ cup vegetable oil
  3 medium onions, finely
    chopped
  2 medium bell peppers,
    finely chopped
  1 celery stalk, finely
    chopped
  1 cup chicken stock
  1 cup green onions,
    chopped
 ½ cup parsley, chopped

★

Maque Choux

Serves 8
Preparation Time:
  45 Minutes

  2 **dozen ears of fresh**
     sweet corn
  1 **cup butter**
  2 **medium onions, finely**
     chopped
  2 **large bell peppers,**
     finely chopped
  6 **large ripe tomatoes,**
     peeled, seeded and
     roughly chopped
  2 **tsps. salt**
  2 **tsps. ground black**
     pepper

Shuck the corn. Working with one cob at a time, hold over a bowl and cut away the kernels in layers (you don't want to end up with whole kernels), then scrape the knife down the cob to "milk" it.

Heat the butter in a Dutch oven or other large, heavy pot over medium-high heat.

Add the onions, bell peppers and tomatoes and sauté until the onions are translucent, about 15 minutes.

Stir in the salt and pepper, then add the corn and the milk from the cobs and stir well. Reduce heat to medium and cook until the corn is tender, about 20 to 30 minutes. If the mixture begins to dry out before the corn is tender, add a little milk and a little more butter.

☆

Pineapple Upside-Down Cake

Butter a 10-inch cast-iron skillet or other heavy, round, ovenproof pan.

     Place the butter and sugar in the bowl of an electric mixer and cream them well. Beat in the eggs. Sift together the flour, baking powder and salt and add to the batter alternating with the milk, in two stages. Gently fold in the vanilla.

     Sprinkle the brown sugar evenly over the bottom of the prepared skillet or pan. Arrange the slices of pineapple in a single layer over the sugar and place a cherry in the center of each. Pour the batter over the pineapple.

     Place the cake in a 350° oven and bake for 40 to 45 minutes, or until a knife or toothpick inserted near the center comes out clean.

     Remove the cake and let it cool completely. Invert onto a cake plate and serve.

Serves 8
Preparation Time:
 1 Hour
Preheat oven to 350°

- ½ cup butter, room temperature
- 1 cup sugar
- 3 eggs, beaten
- 2 cups cake flour, sifted
- 3 tsps. baking powder
- ½ tsp. salt
- ⅔ cup milk
- 1 tsp. vanilla
- 1 cup dark brown sugar
- 8 slices sweetened canned pineapple
- 8 maraschino cherries

☆

ANDREA'S

NORTHERN ITALIAN
3100 19th Street at Ridgelake
Metairie, Louisiana 70002
(504) 834-8583
Lunch and Dinner Monday–Saturday 11 a.m.–10:30 p.m.
Dinner Sunday 3 p.m.–9 p.m.
AVERAGE DINNER FOR TWO: $75

With more than twenty years of creative culinary experience throughout western Europe and the United States, Chef Andrea serves classic Northern Italian cuisine made from Louisiana ingredients.

Tempting appetizer combinations of antipasto are on view on the display table near the entrance to the restaurant. Other superb starters are the fresh Mussels steamed in a white wine sauce or a light tomato broth with fresh spices. The New Orleans turtle soup is simmered in a delicate stock and seasoned with herbs and sherry wine.

Homemade pastas are the specialty ranging from angel hair with salmon and caviar to pesto, crab meat ravioli, linguine and tortellini.

Entree highlights include fresh fillet of trout sautéed in butter and served with mushrooms and artichokes in a meunière sauce, veal topped with jumbo crab meat in a light cream sauce and homemade ravioli stuffed with four cheeses.

RECIPE SECRETS FROM ANDREA'S

Stuffed Artichoke with Crab Meat Louisiane

Risotto Champagne

Harlequin Red Fish

Panéed Alligator

Stuffed Artichoke with Crab Meat Louisiane

Place artichokes in a gallon of boiling water with ½ tsp. salt and two halved lemons. Boil for 12 minutes or until leaves have just begun to get tender. Remove and cool.

Heat the olive oil in a skillet and sauté the onions, garlic, celery, green and red bell pepper and anchovies until the vegetables are tender. Stir in all of the seafood gently, so as not to break up the crab meat. Cook until bubbling.

Add the white wine, thyme, oregano, basil and parsley. Cook until most of the liquid has evaporated or been absorbed. Add the cayenne, bread crumbs and cheese.

Pull out the inner ten or twelve leaves from the inside of the artichoke and spread the other leaves apart. Salt and pepper the artichokes lightly and fill each center with about 2 Tbsps. stuffing mixture.

Stuffed Artichoke Topping

- ¼ cup extra-virgin olive oil
- 2 anchovy fillets, chopped
- 2 sprigs fresh Italian parsley, chopped
- 1 cup chicken stock
- ½ tsp. salt
- Pinch white pepper
- Bread crumbs
- Grated Parmesan cheese

Heat the olive oil in a heavy skillet and sauté the anchovies and parsley for 30 seconds. Add the chicken stock and the salt and white pepper. Bring to a boil, then remove from heat.

Sprinkle artichokes with bread crumbs and cheese. Stand the stuffed artichokes in a skillet. Pour liquid plus 1 cup of water around them and place the skillet in a preheated 400° oven for 10 minutes.

Serves 6
Preparation Time:
30 Minutes
Preheat oven to 400°

- 12 small artichokes, stems removed
- ½ tsp. salt
- 2 lemons, halved
- ½ cup olive oil
- ¼ cup onions, chopped
- 1 Tbsp. garlic, chopped
- 1 stalk celery, coarsely chopped
- ½ cup red and green bell pepper, chopped
- 8 anchovy fillets
- ⅓ cup baby shrimp
- 2 scallops, chopped
- 2 oysters, chopped
- ½ cup lump crab meat
- ½ cup dry white wine
- 5 sprigs fresh thyme leaves, chopped
- 2 sprigs fresh oregano, chopped
- 3 sprigs fresh Italian parsley, chopped
- 2 fresh basil leaves, chopped
- ⅛ tsp. cayenne
- ¼ cup bread crumbs
- ¼ cup Parmesan cheese, grated
- ½ tsp. salt
- Pinch white pepper
- Artichoke topping (recipe follows)

☆

Risotto Champagne

Serves 4
Preparation Time:
  30 Minutes

  ½ **cup sparkling wine**
    (recommend Domaine
    Chandon)
    Generous pinch of
    saffron threads
  ¼ **cup dry vermouth**
  ⅓ **cup chicken stock**
  1 **cup prepared risotto**
    (recipe follows)
  ½ **tsp. butter, softened**
  1 **Tbsp. Parmesan**
    cheese, grated
  1 **Tbsp. roasted pine nuts**

Basic Risotto:
Preheat oven to 450°
  2 **qts. chicken stock**
  8 **Tbsps. butter (1 stick)**
  1 **Tbsp. onion, chopped**
  ½ **Tbsp. garlic, chopped**
  1 **lb. Arborio rice**
  1 **cup dry white wine**
  ½ **tsp. salt**
    Pinch white pepper

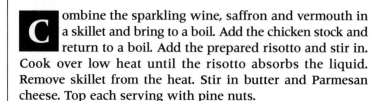

ombine the sparkling wine, saffron and vermouth in a skillet and bring to a boil. Add the chicken stock and return to a boil. Add the prepared risotto and stir in. Cook over low heat until the risotto absorbs the liquid. Remove skillet from the heat. Stir in butter and Parmesan cheese. Top each serving with pine nuts.

Basic Risotto
Bring the chicken stock to a boil in a large saucepan. Heat the butter in a second saucepan (minimum 5-qt. capacity) over medium heat. When it begins bubbling, add the onion and garlic and sauté until the onion is translucent. Increase the heat to high and add the rice. Stir well to coat all the rice with the hot butter. When you see the first hint of browning, stir in the wine and lower the heat.

Pour in the boiling chicken stock and add the salt and pepper. When the ingredients return to a boil, place the pan in a 450° oven for 15 to 20 minutes.

Remove the risotto from the saucepan immediately. Spread it out in a large skillet, pizza pan or sheet pan and allow to cool. Do not let it cool in the saucepan, as it will continue to cook from the heat of the pan.

☆

Harlequin Red Fish

Wash the fish under cold water and pat dry. In a shallow-bottomed bowl combine 1 Tbsp. extra-virgin olive oil, 1 Tbsp. wine, 1 Tbsp. lemon juice, ½ tsp. Worcestershire sauce and a dash of Tabasco. Marinate the fish for 1 to 2 minutes on each side in the marinade. Sprinkle the fillets lightly with salt, pepper, and flour.

Heat 2 Tbsps. olive oil in a hot skillet. Sauté the fish for about 1 minute and turn. Place the skillet in a 400° oven and bake for about 5 minutes. Do not allow the fish to dry out or crack. Remove the fish to serving plates and keep it warm.

To the same skillet, add 2 Tbsps. olive oil over medium heat. Sauté the onion, bell peppers, garlic and crushed red pepper until the onion turns translucent. Add ½ cup wine and bring to a boil. Add the fish stock, 1 Tbsp. lemon juice, oregano, ½ tsp. Worcestershire, tomato and salt. Return to a boil and cook until the peppers have just lost their crispness, but are still al dente.

To serve, drape the peppers and onions across the fish and pour the sauce around the fish.

Serves 4
Preparation Time:
  30 Minutes
Preheat oven to 400°

  4 red fish fillets, 6 to
    8 oz. each
  5 Tbsps. extra-virgin
    olive oil
  ½ cup + 1 Tbsp. dry
    white wine
  2 Tbsps. lemon juice
  1 tsp. Worcestershire
    sauce
    Dash of Tabasco Sauce
    Salt and pepper to
    taste
    Flour for breading
  ½ onion, sliced
  1 cup mixed red, green
    and yellow bell pepper,
    thinly sliced
  1 tsp. garlic, minced
    Pinch of crushed red
    pepper
  1 cup fish stock
  2 sprigs fresh oregano
  1 ripe tomato, peeled
    and seeded, coarsely
    chopped
  ½ tsp. salt

☆

Panéed Alligator

Serves 4
Preparation Time:
  30 Minutes
Preheat oven to 400°

  4 slices alligator loin,
    6 oz. each
    Flour
    Salt
    White pepper
  2 eggs, beaten
    Bread crumbs
  ⅓ cup vegetable oil
    Parmesan cheese,
    grated, for garnish
    Italian parsley for
    garnish

Pound out the alligator slices to double their original size. Dust the alligator with flour, salt and pepper.

Dip the alligator scallops into the beaten eggs, then coat with bread crumbs.

Heat the vegetable oil in a skillet to very hot. Sauté the alligator on one side until lightly browned. Turn the alligator over and place the skillet in a 400° oven for 8 minutes or continue cooking over medium-low heat on the stovetop for 3 minutes more.

Serve the alligator sprinkled with grated Parmesan cheese and Italian parsley.

Cooking Secret: This dish is delicious with the risotto champagne.

ANTOINE'S

FRENCH
713-717 Rue St. Louis
New Orleans, Louisiana 70130
(504) 581-4422
Lunch Monday–Saturday 11:30 a.m.–2 p.m.
Dinner Monday–Saturday 5:30 p.m.–9:30 p.m.
AVERAGE DINNER FOR TWO: $100

Spanning 150 years and five generations, the Alciatore family have been creating dishes and dining excitement for New Orleans and the world. Antoine's creations such as Oysters à La Rockefeller have become classics. The dish was named due to the extreme richness of the sauce and because at the time, the elder Rockefeller was the richest man in world.

Thanks to Chef Antoine, puffed potatoes debuted in the Western Hemisphere. Due to the tardiness of a king, the potatoes needed to be refreshed in hot boiling oil, and, to Antoine's amazement, they puffed up like balloons. Needless to say, the king was delighted and pomme de terre soufflées were born.

Yet Antoine's is today what it was at its inception—an immaculate restaurant serviced by attentive waiters, who speak many tongues because they have learned their vocation on both continents. When you go to Antoine's, located in the historic French Quarter, it is to give your palate an undisturbed treat.

RECIPE SECRETS FROM ANTOINE'S

Oysters Bonne Femme

Shrimp Ravigote

Pommes de Terre au Gratin

Oysters Bonne Femme

Serves 6
Preparation Time:
  1 Hour
Preheat oven to 400°

  36 oysters in their liquor
   3 Tbsps. butter
   3 Tbsps. flour
  ½ cup dry white wine
  ¾ cup green onions,
     chopped
   1 Tbsp. parsley, minced
     Salt and white pepper
     to taste
   1 cup lump crab meat
   2 Tbsps. Swiss cheese,
     grated
   2 Tbsps. Romano cheese,
     grated
   2 Tbsps. mozzarella
     cheese, grated
  ⅓ cup bread crumbs

Place the oysters in a small saucepan with their liquor and simmer for 10 to 12 minutes or until cooked but not soft. Strain the liquid from the oysters (about 1¾ cups) and set aside.

Melt the butter in a saucepan and stir in the flour. Cook the flour and butter together for 2 minutes, stirring occasionally, until the mixture becomes foamy. Add the reserved oyster liquor, the white wine, green onions, parsley, salt and pepper to taste. Bring to a boil, then turn down to a simmer and continue cooking for 15 minutes.

Fold in the oysters and crab meat, being careful not to break them up. Adjust the seasoning if necessary.

In a separate bowl, blend the grated cheeses and bread crumbs.

To serve, spoon the warm oyster and crab meat mixture into a 1-qt. soufflé dish or 6 individual half-cup soufflé dishes. Sprinkle the cheese and bread crumb mixture evenly over the top.

Bake for 20 minutes in a 400° oven or until the cheese is melted and begins to brown. Remove from the oven and serve.

Shrimp Ravigote

Mix together the bell pepper, green onion, pimiento, chopped anchovy and mayonnaise.
Gently fold in the shrimp until the sauce lightly coats them.

To serve, place the shrimp on a bed of watercress. Garnish with tomato wedges and anchovy fillets.

Cooking Secret: Crab meat may be substituted for shrimp.

Serves 8
Preparation Time:
** 20 Minutes**

½ green bell pepper,
   minced
½ bunch green onion,
   minced
½ medium pimiento,
   chopped
8 anchovy fillets,
   chopped fine
2 cups mayonnaise
3 lbs. shrimp, boiled and
   peeled
1 bunch watercress
1 tomato cut into
   8 wedges
   Anchovy fillets for
   garnish

☆

Pommes de Terre au Gratin

Serves 6
Preparation Time:
  30 Minutes
Preheat oven to 400°

  2 lbs. potatoes
  1 Tbsp. salt
  2 cups béchamel sauce
    (recipe follows)
    Salt and white pepper
    to taste
  3 Tbsps. Swiss cheese,
    grated
  3 Tbsps. Romano cheese,
    grated
  3 Tbsps. mozzarella
    cheese, grated
  ¼ cup bread crumbs

Béchamel Sauce:
  4 Tbsps. butter
  2 Tbsps. flour
  1½ cups warm scalded
    milk
    Salt and ground white
    pepper to taste

Wash and peel the potatoes. Place them in the bottom of a large saucepan and add enough boiling water to cover. Add 1 Tbsp. of salt, cover the pan and continue boiling the potatoes until they are tender when pierced with a sharp knife. Remove the potatoes from the water and cut into ½-inch cubes.

Combine the potato cubes with the béchamel sauce, being careful not to break them up. Add salt and pepper if needed.

Spoon the potato mixture into six small individual oven-proof dishes. Mix together the cheeses and the bread crumbs and sprinkle on top.

Place in a 400° oven until the cheese is melted and the top begins to brown.

Béchamel Sauce
Melt 2 Tbsps. butter and add flour over low heat. Stir and cook until the mixture becomes foamy. Do not allow to brown. Stir in the milk and bring to a boil, then reduce heat to a simmer. Add the salt and pepper to taste. Remove from the heat and dot top of sauce with 2 Tbsps. of butter to prevent a film from forming.

☆

ARNAUD'S

CREOLE AND CONTINENTAL CUISINE
813 Bienville Stree
New Orleans, Louisiana
(800) 453-1020
(504) 523-5433
Lunch Monday–Friday 11:30 a.m.–2:30 p.m.
Dinner Daily 6 p.m.–10 p.m.
AVERAGE DINNER FOR TWO: $85

I n 1918, Arnaud Cazenave opened the doors of Arnaud's and a legend began. Dubbed the "Count" by his friends, he spent thirty years building the restaurant into one of the finest dining establishments in the United States. Upon the "Count's" death, his daughter, Germaine Wells, took over the restaurant. Archie Casbarian, today's proprietor, was her hand-picked successor, and took over in 1978.

Archie and Jane Casbarian, award-winning restaurateurs, have taken Arnaud's tradition to new heights. The menu is a combination of French and Creole cookery featuring signature dishes such as Shrimp Arnaud, which is Gulf shrimp marinated in the famous tangy Creole Remoulade Sauce. Oyster Bienville is Arnaud's creation of shrimp and mushrooms in a White Wine Sauce. The Speckled Trout Meunière is a crispy fried filet of speckled trout served with a Creole Meunière Sauce and the Pompano en Croute is pompano filets baked in puff pastry with scallop mousse then served on a bed of Green Peppercorn Sauce. The Breast of Duck Ellen is a sautéed duck breast served with marinated blueberries and Port Wine Sauce. Arnaud's offers a variety of fish, fowl, veal, seafood and steaks on their menu.

In a city famous for great dining, music and festivity at all hours of the day and night, Sunday brunch and jazz are a great combination at Arnaud's with diners listening to a live New Orleans-style jazz band.

RECIPE SECRETS FROM ARNAUD'S

Oysters Bienville

Watercress à la Germaine

Arnaud's Shrimp Creole

Stuffed Rock Cornish Game Hens with Bordelaise Sauce

Café Brûlot

Oysters Bienville

Serves 4
Preparation Time:
  40 Minutes
(note refrigeration time)
Preheat oven to 500°

²⁄₃ cup mushrooms, finely
   chopped
 1 Tbsp. vegetable oil
 4 Tbsps. unsalted butter
1½ tsps. garlic, finely
   minced
 1 Tbsp. shallots, finely
   chopped
½ lb. boiled shrimp,
   finely diced
 1 Tbsp. flour
½ cup brandy
½ cup heavy cream
 6 Tbsps. Romano cheese,
   grated
 4 Tbsps. dry bread
   crumbs
¼ cup parsley, finely
   minced
 1 tsp. salt
 1 tsp. ground white
   pepper
½ tsp. cayenne pepper
   Milk, optional
24 oysters on the half
   shell, drained
 4 pans rock salt

I n a large, heavy saucepan, sauté the chopped mushrooms quickly in the vegetable oil. Remove from pan and set aside.

In the same pan, melt the unsalted butter and sauté the garlic and shallots, stirring frequently until soft. Add the diced shrimp, then sprinkle in the flour. Stir all together, add the reserved mushrooms. Deglaze the pan with the brandy while stirring constantly. Stir in the heavy cream and cook until smooth. Add the Romano cheese, dry bread crumbs, parsley, salt, pepper and cayenne. A small amount of milk may be added if the mixture is too thick.

Remove from heat and allow to cool. Refrigerate for about 1½ hours.

Thirty minutes before you plan to bake the oysters, place the pans of rock salt in a preheated 500° oven.

Wash oyster shells well, pat dry. Place oysters on shells, putting six in each pan of rock salt. Spoon one heaping tablespoon of sauce over each oyster. Bake for 15 to 18 minutes until well browned.

☆

Watercress à la Germaine

Divide the watercress among serving plates and top with the mushrooms. Drizzle the dressing over the salad and garnish each plate with cherry tomatoes.

Using a mixer at low speed, blend the mayonnaise, sour cream and cream cheese for 3 minutes. Add the crushed peppercorns, green onions, Worcestershire and Tabasco. Blend for another 3 minutes. Season to taste with salt and white pepper.

* Creole cream cheese, a single large curd surrounded by cream, is a unique New Orleans product. If it's not available in your area, a good substitute is heavy cream poured over either farmer cheese or large-curd cottage cheese.

Serves 4
Preparation Time:
  15 Minutes

  3 **bunches watercress,**
    cleaned
  2 **cups mushrooms,**
    sliced
  ¾ **cup watercress**
    dressing (recipe
    follows)
  12 **cherry tomatoes**

Watercress Dressing:
  ½ **cup mayonnaise**
  ¼ **cup sour cream**
  ⅛ **cup Creole cream**
    cheese*
  1¼ **tsps. green**
    peppercorns, crushed
  2 **Tbsps. green onions or**
    scallions, chopped
  1¼ **tsps. Worcestershire**
    sauce
    Dash of Tabasco Sauce
    Salt and white pepper
    to taste

Arnaud's Shrimp Creole

Serves 4
Preparation Time:
  30 Minutes

  4 Tbsps. virgin olive oil
  3 lbs. boiled shrimp
  3 cups Creole Sauce
    (recipe follows)
    Salt and freshly
    ground black pepper
    to taste
4½ cups white rice,
    cooked
  ½ cup fresh parsley,
    chopped

Creole Sauce:
  2 Tbsps. olive oil
  1 cup white onion,
    chopped
  ½ cup green pepper,
    diced
1½ cups celery, chopped
  ½ cup fresh parsley,
    chopped
  1 garlic clove, chopped
  2 cups veal stock
1¼ tsps. chicken base or
    bouillon
  1 bouquet garni*
  ½ cup diced tomatoes
1½ cups tomato purée
    Salt and freshly
    ground pepper to taste
    Tabasco to taste
    Cayenne pepper to
    taste

Heat the olive oil in a skillet over high heat. Add the shrimp and stir for a minute, until they are heated through. Add the Creole sauce and bring to a boil. Reduce the heat and simmer for 3 minutes. Season to taste with salt and pepper.

For the sauce: Heat the olive oil over high heat, then add the onion, green pepper, celery and parsley. Stir and cook for about 2 minutes, then add the garlic. Stir in the veal stock and chicken base or bouillon, add the bouquet garni, diced tomatoes and tomato purée and bring to a boil. Reduce the heat, allow to simmer for 10 minutes. Season to taste with the salt, pepper, Tabasco and cayenne.

To serve, divide the rice among dinner plates and spoon the shrimp and sauce over each serving. Sprinkle with chopped parsley. Serve at once.

* Bouquet garni is comprised of ½ bunch parsley, 3 bay leaves, 1 bunch fresh thyme and 1 stalk celery, tied together with butcher's twine. Leave a long tail of twine and tie the bouquet to the handle of the pot.

Stuffed Rock Cornish Game Hens with Bordelaise Sauce

In a large mixing bowl, combine all the ingredients and mix to a smooth, mousse-like consistency. Refrigerate until ready to use.

Stuffed Rock Cornish Game Hens
Divide stuffing among the four game hens, which have been seasoned with salt and pepper. Wrap each stuffed bird in a slice of bacon. Place in a roasting pan. Pour veal stock over, cover and braise in the oven for about 45 minutes. When done, remove hens to a warm platter, discarding the bacon.

  1 cup mushrooms, quartered
  4 Tbsps. clarified butter
  2 whole tomatoes, peeled, chopped
      Bordelaise Sauce (recipe follows)
      Salt and white pepper to taste
  1 Tbsp. parsley, chopped
      Cherry tomatoes for garnish
      Parsley sprigs for garnish

In a saucepan, sauté the mushrooms quickly in clarified butter. Then add the chopped tomatoes and Bordelaise Sauce. Heat through and adjust the seasonings, adding chopped parsley.

    To serve, pour sauce over hens on a large serving platter. Garnish with cherry tomatoes and parsley sprigs. Serve immediately.

Bordelaise Sauce
Recipe follows on next page.

Cooking Secret: To save time make the stuffing in advance and refrigerate. The Bordelaise Sauce may also be made a bit ahead.

Serves 4
Preparation Time:
  1½ Hours
Preheat oven to 400°

Stuffing:
  4 **Tbsps. shallots,**
      chopped
  ¾ cup ruby port
  2 **large eggs**
  ¼ cup heavy cream
  1 **Tbsp. parsley, chopped**
  ¼ cup pork tenderloin,
      finely minced
  1 **cup veal top round,**
      finely minced
  2 **Tbsps. fat back, finely**
      minced
  ½ tsp. crushed thyme
      Salt and freshly
      ground pepper to taste

Stuffed Rock Cornish
Game Hens:
  4 **Cornish game hens**
      Salt and freshly
      ground black pepper
      to taste
  4 **slices bacon**
  1 **qt. veal stock**

☆

Bordelaise Sauce

Preparation Time:
  20 Minutes

  2 **Tbsps. butter**
¼ **cup shallots, chopped**
  1 **cup red wine**
  1 **bouquet garni***
  1 **whole clove**
  1 **black peppercorn**
  1 **bay leaf**
½ **garlic clove**
  1 **qt. veal stock**
  1 **Tbsp. glacé de viande†**
    Salt and freshly
      ground pepper to taste

Melt the butter in a pan over high heat, then add the shallots and cook until translucent. Add the red wine and bring to a boil, then add the bouquet garni, clove, peppercorn, bay leaf, garlic and veal stock. Reduce heat and simmer until the volume is reduced by half and coats a spoon. Stir in the glacé de viande. Strain, then season to taste with salt and pepper.

* Bouquet garni is ½ bunch parsley, 3 bay leaves, 1 bunch fresh thyme and 1 stalk celery, tied together with butcher's twine. Leave a long tail of twine and tie the bouquet to the handle of the pot.

†Glacé de viande is French for "meat glaze," made by boiling meat juices until they are reduced to a thick syrup. It is used to add flavor and color to sauces.

☆

Café Brûlot

Combine the cinnamon, cloves, fruit peel and sugar lumps over heat in a brûlot bowl or chafing dish and crush them together, using the back of the ladle. Add the brandy and Curaçao and mix well. When the mixture begins to boil, ignite and keep stirring to dissolve the sugar. Add the black coffee very gradually. Ladle into special brûlot demitasse cups.

The traditional brûlot ladle has a strainer to catch the spices. When using an ordinary ladle, be careful to fill it with only the liquid.

Serve the Café Brûlot as a delightful dessert on its own or with a dessert. Café Brûlot is a festive addition to a special dinner or any occasion.

Serves 4
Preparation Time:
  10 Minutes

  1 **cinnamon stick**
  6 **whole cloves**
  ¼ **cup orange peel, slivered**
  ¼ **cup lemon peel, slivered**
  3 **lumps sugar**
  ½ **cup brandy**
  2 **Tbsps. Curaçao (orange liqueur)**
  3 **cups hot, strong black coffee**

☆

BACCO

ITALIAN with a New Orleans Twist
310 Charles Street
New Orleans, Louisiana 70130
(504) 522-2426
http://www.bacco.com
Dinner Nightly 6 p.m.–10 p.m.
Lunch Monday–Saturday 11:30 a.m.–2:30 p.m.
Brunch Sunday 10:30 a.m.–3 p.m.
AVERAGE DINNER FOR TWO: $75

Simple, gusty food with the intrinsic taste of fresh ingredients is what Bacco delivers, along with caring service and easy comfort. Located in the French Quarter between Bienville and Conti streets, its airy interior has the feel of an Italian trattoria, simultaneously blending classy and casual.

The atmosphere is completely in keeping with the food's strong Italian base, infused with local nuances, rendering Bacco both continental and local. Rounding out the exquisite menu are a thoroughly wonderful wine list, hearty loaves of homemade bread, a most decadent dessert list and a Sunday Jazz Brunch.

Menu highlights include a delicate seafood Cioppino served with Grilled Tuscan Bread, Hickory Grilled Yellowfin Tuna perched on a Red Pepper Coulis with a Vidalia Onion Relish and the Rosemary and Garlic Marinated Pork Tenderloin served with Mashed Potatoes and a Sweet-and-Sour Prune Sauce.

RECIPE SECRETS FROM BACCO

Risotto Jambalaya

Gulf Fish with Creole Tomato Relish

Bacco Crawfish Cannelloni

Risotto Jambalaya

Prepare risotto according to package directions.
Heat the oil in a sauté pan over medium-high heat.
Add the onion, and sauté until soft. Add the bell pepper, and cook until it softens, then add the garlic.

Add the shrimp, andouille sausage and chicken. When the shrimp turns opaque, add the remaining ingredients. Stir with a wooden spoon until creamy. Add more stock if needed.

Adjust seasonings to taste and serve.

Serves 4
Preparation Time:
  30 Minutes

  3 oz. risotto
  2 Tbsps. oil
  2 Tbsps. yellow onion,
    diced
  2 Tbsps. red bell pepper,
    diced
  ¼ tsp. garlic, chopped
  4 large shrimp, deveined
  2 oz. andouille sausage,
    grilled and sliced
  2 oz. chicken breast,
    grilled and sliced
  ¼ cup chicken stock,
    heated
  3 Tbsps. tomato sauce
  ¼ tsp. Creole seasoning
    Salt and pepper to
    taste

Gulf Fish with Creole Tomato Relish

Serves 4
Preparation Time:
5 Minutes
(note marinating time)

1 Tbsp. each fresh basil,
  parsley and oregano
½ cup extra virgin olive
  oil
  Salt and pepper to
  taste
4 fish fillets (red
  snapper, grouper,
  speckled trout, redfish
  or flounder)
¾ cup Creole Tomato
  Relish (recipe follows)
  Lemon wedges for
  garnish

Creole Tomato Relish:
⅓ cup extra virgin olive
  oil
2 Tbsps. garlic, sliced
1½ lbs. crawfish tails
3½ lbs. tomatoes, cored
  and diced
½ cup red onion, finely
  diced
  Pinch of crushed red
  pepper
3 Tbsps. seasoned rice
  vinegar
2 tsps. basil chiffonade
1½ tsps. kosher salt
½ lemon, juiced
  Black pepper, freshly
  ground

lace the herbs, oil, salt and pepper in a blender and purée. Pour the mixture over the fish fillets and let stand for 30 minutes.

Grill or broil the fish to the desired doneness.

Place the Creole Tomato Relish on top of the cooked fish. Garnish with lemon wedges and serve.

Creole Tomato Relish

Place the olive oil in a large sauté pan over medium heat. Add the garlic and cook to a golden brown.

Add the crawfish, toss well, and remove from the heat when they are cooked through.

In a large bowl, put the tomatoes, onion, red pepper, vinegar, basil, salt, lemon juice and black pepper. Add the crawfish and toss together. Let sit for 30 minutes to intensify flavors.

☆

Bacco Crawfish Cannelloni

In a sauté pan, sweat down the garlic, onion and leek until soft.

Add the corn, tomatoes, crawfish and Creole seasoning and sauté for 2 minutes over medium heat.

Add the cream and season with salt and pepper. Cook for 10 minutes over medium-low heat. Add the green onions and let cool.

When filling is cool, place in cannelloni shells and serve with your favorite sauce.

Cooking Secret: Lasagna may be substituted for cannelloni shells.

Serves 4
Preparation Time:
  30 Minutes

2 Tbsps. garlic, chopped
1 yellow onion, diced
1 large leek, white part only, diced
4 ears corn, roasted, shaved off the cobs
2 cups tomatoes, roasted, rough chopped
1 lb. crawfish tails
  Creole seasoning to taste
1½ cups heavy cream
  Salt and pepper to taste
1 bunch green onions, thinly sliced
  Cannelloni shells (precooked), enough to serve 4
  Pasta sauce of your choice

BELLA LUNA

CONTINENTAL AND SOUTHWESTERN CUISINE
914 North Peters Street
New Orleans, Louisiana
(504) 529-1583
Dinner Monday–Saturday 6 p.m.–10:30 p.m.
Dinner Sunday 6 p.m.–9:30 p.m.
AVERAGE DINNER FOR TWO: $75

T he moon...the stars...the river. Wonderful surroundings and great, great food. Bella Luna is located in the French Quarter, where Dumaine meets the river.

The eclectic menu has gained rave reviews, both from the critics and knowledgeable New Orleans restaurant-goers. Too varied to be easily pigeon-holed, the menu appetizingly blends New Orleans, Continental and even Southwestern specialties.

Menu highlights include Freshly Steamed Maine Lobster Tossed with Calamari-Ink Colored Fettuccine; Roma Tomatoes, Fresh Basil and Saffron Aioli; Sautéed Redfish in a Sweet Basil Pesto Crust Served with Wilted Spinach; a Tasso Stuffed Shrimp with Persimmon Habañero Salsa and Homegrown Cilantro; and Oven Roasted Quail Stuffed with Crawfish and Crabmeat over a White Chocolate Tomatillo Salsa. The extensive wine menu includes selections from California, France and Italy.

RECIPE SECRETS FROM BELLA LUNA

Creole Crab Cakes with Pico de Gallo

Lobster Medallions with Vanilla Vinaigrette

Baked Snapper with Grilled Pineapple

Pecan Breaded Pork Chops with Beer Sauce

Mint Chocolate Ice Soufflé

Creole Crab Cakes with Pico de Gallo

Sauté the celery and onion in a hot skillet with a little olive oil or butter and then let them cool. After cubing the French bread, mix the remaining ingredients together (keep a little of the bread crumbs aside to coast hands when forming the cakes).

Form the crab cakes to the desired size, and sauté them in the skillet with olive oil for 2 to 3 minutes on each side.

For the pico de gallo: Mix all ingredients together in a large mixing bowl. Let set for 1 hour. Re-season to taste.

Serves 4
Preparation Time:
  40 Minutes
(note refrigeration time)

- 2 celery stalks, finely diced
- 1 large onion, finely diced
  Olive oil
- 4 cups French bread, ¼-inch cubes
- 1 lb. crab meat, shelled
- ½ red bell pepper, finely diced
- ½ green bell pepper, finely diced
- 2 Tbsps. dry mustard
- 1 tsp. cayenne pepper
- 1 Tbsp. garlic powder
- 1 Tbsp. onion powder
- 3 egg whites
- 2 cups bread crumbs
- ½ cup mayonnaise

Pico de Gallo:
- 1 bunch cilantro, finely chopped
- 1 large red onion, finely chopped
- 3 serrano chile peppers, finely chopped
- 1 lb. tomatoes, diced
  Juice of 3 limes
  Cumin to taste
  Salt and pepper to taste

☆

Lobster Medallions with Vanilla Vinaigrette

Serves 4
Preparation Time:
   15 Minutes
(note refrigeration time)

   1 vanilla bean
   ¼ cup sherry vinegar
   ½ cup grape seed oil
      Salt, pepper and sugar
      to taste
   2 shallots, finely diced
   ½ cup arugula
   ½ red onion, sliced
   1 tomato, sliced
   1 avocado, sliced
   1 lobster, steamed, about
      1½ lbs.
      Pinch of chervil

C ut the vanilla bean in half the long way and scrape out the seeds. Mix the seeds with the vinegar and oil and season with salt, pepper and sugar. Add the shallots and let the vinaigrette sit for 4 hours to intensify the vanilla flavor.

Arrange the arugula, onions, tomatoes and avocados on a plate. Place the lobster medallion and claw on top. Drizzle the vinaigrette over the lobster and salad. Garnish with fresh chervil flakes.

Baked Snapper with Grilled Pineapple

S eason the snapper with juice from 1 lemon, salt, pepper and Worcestershire. Let rest for 10 minutes, then remove from liquid. Sprinkle with thyme and rosemary.

In a sauté pan, melt ½ stick of butter over medium heat until golden brown. Add the snapper and sauté for 2 minutes on each side. Finish in the oven at 375° for 10 to 12 minutes.

Sauté the shallots in 1 Tbsp. butter, then add the vermouth, cream and orange juice. Reduce until ⅓ of the liquid remains, then add pink peppercorns and whisk in the remaining butter. Remove from the heat until ready to use. Do not let it cool down completely. Immediately before serving add the finely chopped basil.

Clean the pineapples and cut in half from the top to the bottom, then cut in to ¼-inch-thick slices.

Mix together the rice wine vinegar, mint and garlic and marinate the pineapple slices for a few minutes. Remove from the liquid, then season with salt and pepper and grill on both sides with olive oil long enough to create grill marks. The pineapple can now be placed on the dinner plate.

On the plate, place the grilled pineapple, topped with the snapper and lightly cover with the citrus peppercorn sauce. Garnish with fresh basil and the remaining lemons, cut in quarters.

Serves 6
Preparation Time:
  45 Minutes
Preheat oven to 375°

- 6 snapper filets, 6 to 8 oz. each
- 4 whole lemons
  Salt and pepper to taste
- 3 Tbsps. Worcestershire sauce
- 2 Tbsps. lemon thyme, chopped
- 1 Tbsp. rosemary, chopped
- 1 stick butter
- 3 shallots, finely chopped
- ¼ cup vermouth
- ¼ cup whipping cream
  Juice from 20 oranges
- 3 Tbsps. pink peppercorns
- 2 Tbsps. basil, finely chopped
- 2 fresh ripe pineapples
- ¼ cup seasoned rice wine vinegar
- 2 Tbsps. mint, chopped
- 1 tsp. garlic, chopped
- 2 tsps. olive oil

☆

Pecan Breaded Pork Chops with Beer Sauce

Serves 6
Preparation Time:
  30 Minutes
Preheat oven to 350°

  1 cup pecans
  1 cup bread crumbs
  1 tsp. dry mustard
  1 tsp. celery salt
    Salt and pepper to
    taste
  6 pork chops
  1 cup flour
  1 egg, beaten
  4 Tbsps. butter

Beer Sauce:
  1 cup onions
  1 tsp. garlic
  1 Tbsp. caraway seeds
  1 bottle beer
  2 cups demi-glace
    Salt and pepper to
    taste

Mix together the pecans, bread crumbs and seasonings in a food processor. Dust the pork chops with flour, then dip in egg wash. Bread with the pecan mixture. Sauté the pork chops in butter on both sides until brown, then bake in a 350° oven for 15 minutes until fully cooked.

For the sauce: Sauté the onions, garlic and caraway seeds over medium heat. Deglaze with the beer and demi-glace and cook for 15 minutes. Finish with salt and pepper to taste. Pour over top of hot pecan-breaded pork chops.

Mint Chocolate Ice Soufflé

Whisk together the egg yolks, eggs and powdered sugar over a double boiler. Then sit it on a bed of ice and whisk until it is cooled. After the mixture is cool, add the schnapps, mint and chocolate. Then fold in the whipped cream.

Place the mixture in a mold and place in the freezer. Serve frozen.

Serves 4
Preparation Time:
20 Minutes
(note freezing time)

10 egg yolks
2 eggs
1½ cups powdered sugar
½ cup peppermint
schnapps
3 Tbsps. fresh mint,
chopped
½ cup chocolate shavings
1 qt. whipped cream

☆

BIZOU

FRENCH-CREOLE CUISINE
701 St. Charles Avenue
New Orleans, Louisiana 70130
(504) 524-4114
Dinner Monday–Saturday 6 p.m.–1 p.m.
Lunch Monday–Friday 11 a.m.–4 p.m.
AVERAGE DINNER FOR TWO: $60

National accolades are rare, even in New Orleans, but not for Chef Daniel Bonnot, who has already made Bizou (a variation of the French word for "little kiss") a local favorite.
Located on historic St. Charles Avenue in downtown New Orleans, Bizou's luxuriant atmosphere is created with rose-colored walls that are punctuated by original large-scale artworks and wrought-iron chandeliers descending from the high ceilings.

If the decor sounds stylish and sophisticated, the menu is more of the same, only better. The large, appealing menu is a dazzling display of culinary rejuvenation of the French-Creole tradition which gives this top eatery true distinction. The difficulty lies in settling on an order.

RECIPE SECRETS FROM BIZOU

Escargot Riviera

Crawfish Beignets with Tartar Sauce

Salmon Primavera

Escargot Riviera

Slice the baguette lengthwise and toast on both sides. Cut into 24 croutons.

Sauté the tomatoes, half the shallots, bouquet garni, wine and 2 cloves of garlic. Cover and cook for 1 hour.

In a mixing bowl, combine the goat cheese, cream cheese, thyme, capers, 1 Tbsp. parsley and egg yolk and mix well. Set mixture aside.

Sauté the snails, butter and remaining parsley and garlic over low heat. Add the Ricard and flambé. Remove from heat. Set aside.

Spread the cheese mixture on each crouton. Top with the tomatoes, then the snails. Cover with aïoli or mayonnaise and season to taste.

Bake in 375° oven for 15 minutes.

Serves 6
Preparation Time:
  1½ Hours
Preheat oven to 375°

- 1 **French baguette**
- 1 **lb. fresh tomatoes**
- 4 **Tbsps. fresh shallots**
- 1 **bouquet garni (herb trio of parsley, thyme and bay leaf tied together with a celery stalk or placed in cheesecloth bag)**
- ½ **cup white wine**
- 4 **cloves garlic**
- 4 **oz. fresh goat cheese**
- 2 **oz. fresh cream cheese**
- 1 **pinch thyme**
- 1 **tsp. capers, chopped**
- 2 **Tbsps. parsley, chopped**
- 1 **egg yolk**
- 24 **snails**
- 2 **Tbsps. butter**
- ½ **oz. Ricard (licorice-flavored apéritif)**
- ⅓ **cup aïoli or mayonnaise**
  Salt and pepper to taste

Crawfish Beignets with Tartar Sauce

Yield: 28 beignets
Preparation Time:
  45 Minutes

  1 cup flour
  1 tsp. baking powder
  1 cup water
  1 tsp. garlic, chopped
  1 pimiento
  3 green onions, chopped
  4 drops Tabasco Sauce
  8 oz. cooked crawfish
    tails, roughly chopped
    Salt to taste

Tartar Sauce:
  2 egg yolks
  1 tsp. Dijon mustard
  1 cup olive oil
  1 tsp. chopped pickle
    (cornichon)
  4 hard-boiled eggs,
    chopped
  1 tsp. parsley, chopped
  2 Tbsps. capers
  ½ tsp. paprika
  ½ tsp. cayenne
    Salt and pepper to
    taste

I n a bowl, mix ingredients in order listed. Cover the bowl with a damp towel and set aside for 30 minutes.
Drop mixture by spoonfuls into 365° oil and fry until golden brown, about 4 to 6 minutes.

Drain and serve hot with a lemon wedge and Tartar Sauce (recipe follows).

Tartar Sauce
In a medium-sized bowl, mix together the egg yolks and Dijon mustard. Slowly add the olive oil. Mix to the consistency of mayonnaise. Add the pickle, eggs, parsley, capers, paprika and cayenne. Season to taste.

Serve with Crawfish Beignets as a dipping sauce.

Salmon Primavera

Sauté the salmon steaks in heated olive oil over medium heat. Cook the salmon on both sides until medium-rare. Remove the salmon from the pan to a serving dish.

In the same pan, sauté all the fruit for approximately 3 minutes. Add the green onion, red onion and tomatoes and cook until tomatoes are soft. Add the white wine and deglaze. Sauté for 2 minutes longer and add the butter.

When the butter has melted, pour the mixture over the salmon steaks and sprinkle with fresh cilantro.

Serves 4
Preparation Time:
  20 Minutes

  4 salmon steaks, 6 oz. each
  4 Tbsps. olive oil
  2 mangoes, peeled and sliced
  2 apples, peeled and sliced
  2 pears, peeled and sliced
  2 Tbsps. green onion, chopped
  2 Tbsps. red onion, chopped
  2 tomatoes, chopped
  $\frac{1}{2}$ cup white wine
  8 Tbsps. butter (1 stick)
  $\frac{1}{3}$ cup fresh cilantro leaves, chopped

☆

BRIGTSEN'S RESTAURANT

CAJUN
723 Dante Street
New Orleans, Louisiana 70118
(504) 861-7610
Dinner Tuesday–Saturday 5:30 p.m.–10 p.m.
AVERAGE DINNER FOR TWO: $80

L ocated on a quiet street in the Carrollton section of New Orleans, Brigtsen's occupies a converted shotgun cottage built in the 1850s. Simply and tastefully decorated with antiques, chintz, lace curtains and slowly turning fans hanging from high ceilings, Brigtsen's welcomes guests with all the charm and warmth for which the Deep South is known.

Chef Frank Brigtsen's signature dishes are dedicated to infusing the Creole-Acadian tradition of cooking with a constant stream of innovation, using unusual ingredients and seasonings. Unlike many chefs who delegate responsibility or lend their name to several restaurants, Frank still spends five nights a week in the kitchen, where he personally cooks most of the dinners. The result is a dining experience that the San Francisco Chronicle and Zagat Survey have called "the most exciting in New Orleans."

Main courses include a generous variety of local seafood as well as Panéed Rabbit with a Sesame Crust, Andouille Cornbread-Stuffed Chicken or Grilled Beef Tournedos with Tasso Marchand du Vin Sauce.

Not surprisingly, the culinary community has praised and awarded Brigtsen's repeatedly for innovative, expertly prepared cuisine.

RECIPE SECRETS FROM BRIGTSEN'S

Gratin of Oysters, Spinach and Shiitake Mushrooms with Brie

Butternut Shrimp Bisque

Blackened Yellowfin Tuna with Smoked Corn Sauce and Red Bean Salsa

Smothered Boneless Pork Chops with Lentils

Gratin of Oysters, Spinach and Shiitake Mushrooms with Brie

I n a mixing bowl, combine the bread crumbs, Parmesan, Romano, melted butter and paprika. Mix well and set aside.

Heat the cream in a heavy saucepan over low heat. Add the Brie, salt and cayenne. Cook, stirring occasionally, until the cheese is completely melted, 2 to 3 minutes. Strain and set aside.

Heat the softened butter in a large skillet over medium-high heat. Add the mushrooms and green onions and cook, stirring constantly, for 1 to 2 minutes. Add the oysters and spinach and cook, stirring constantly, for 1 minute. Add the Brie-and-cream mixture and bring to a boil.

Divide the mixture evenly among 4 shallow casserole dishes and top each dish with bread-crumb-and-cheese mixture.

Place under the broiler and cook until golden brown and bubbly, 2 to 3 minutes. Serve immediately.

Serves 4
Preparation Time:
  20 Minutes
Preheat broiler

- 3 Tbsps. French bread crumbs, finely ground
- 2 Tbsps. Parmesan cheese, grated
- 2 Tbsps. Romano cheese, grated
- 1 Tbsp. unsalted butter, melted
- ¼ tsp. hot Hungarian paprika
- 1 cup heavy whipping cream
- ¼ lb. Brie, diced into 1-inch pieces
- ½ tsp. salt
  Pinch cayenne pepper
- 1 Tbsp. unsalted butter, softened
- 1½ cups shiitake mushrooms, thinly sliced
- ¼ cup thinly sliced green onions
- 24 Louisiana oysters, freshly shucked
- 1½ cups fresh spinach, chopped

☆

Butternut Shrimp Bisque

Serves 6
Preparation Time:
  45 Minutes

  3 Tbsps. butter
  2 cups yellow onions,
    diced
  1 bay leaf
  4 cups butternut squash,
    peeled, de-seeded and
    diced into ½-inch
    cubes
  2 cups fresh shrimp,
    peeled (reserve heads
    and shells for stock)
2¼ tsps. salt
  ⅛ tsp. cayenne pepper,
    ground
  ⅛ tsp. white pepper,
    ground
  ½ cup shrimp stock
  6 cups heavy whipping
    cream

Heat the butter in a heavy saucepan over medium-high heat. Add the onions and bay leaf and cook, stirring constantly, until the onions become soft and clear, 3 to 4 minutes. Reduce the heat to medium and add the butternut squash. Cook this mixture, stirring occasionally, until the squash begins to soften, 6 to 8 minutes.

Reduce the heat to low and add the shrimp, salt, cayenne and white pepper. Cook, stirring occasionally, until the shrimp turn pink, 2 to 3 minutes.

Prepare the stock by placing the shrimp heads and shells in a saucepan and covering with cold water. Bring to a boil, simmer for 5 minutes and strain. Add the shrimp stock to the soup and cook, stirring occasionally, for 6 to 8 minutes. If the mixture begins to stick to the pan, scrape it with a spoon and continue cooking. This will intensify the taste of the bisque.

Transfer the squash mixture to a food processor and purée. Return the puréed squash to the saucepan, add the cream and bring to a boil. Reduce heat to low and simmer for 2 to 3 minutes. Serve immediately.

Blackened Yellowfin Tuna with Smoked Corn Sauce and Red Bean Salsa

In small saucepan, put the red beans and water. Bring to a boil over high heat. Reduce heat to medium-low and cook until the beans are tender, 50 to 60 minutes. When cooked, strain and set aside.

While the beans are cooking, roast the vegetables for the salsa. Preheat the broiler and place the bell peppers, red onion, tomato and jalapeño pepper in a shallow baking pan. Brush each vegetable with a little olive oil. Cook directly under the broiler until the outsides of the vegetables are completely charred, 3 to 5 minutes. Remove the vegetables from the broiler and cover the pan with aluminum foil. Let rest for 10 minutes.

Peel and de-seed the vegetables. Dice the bell peppers, onion and tomato into ¼-inch pieces. Chop the jalapeño pepper very finely.

In a mixing bowl, put the cooked red beans, roasted vegetables and all remaining ingredients. Blend well and refrigerate for at least 1 hour before serving.

Cooking Secret: The red bean salsa and smoked corn sauce are also delicious with grilled tuna.

Recipe continues on next page.

Serves 6
Preparation Time:
 1½ Hours
(note marinating time)
Preheat broiler

Salsa:
 ½ cup small red beans
 4 cups water
 ½ large red bell pepper
 ½ large yellow bell
  pepper
 ½ medium red onion,
  peeled
 1 large, ripe tomato
 1 large jalapeño pepper
 1 Tbsp. olive oil
 2 tsps. white vinegar
 1 tsp. salt
 ½ tsp. fresh garlic,
  minced
 ½ tsp. Tabasco Sauce

Smoked Corn Sauce:

- 2 Tbsps. unsalted butter
- 1 cup yellow onion, finely diced
- 3 cups fresh yellow corn, smoked and cut off the cob*
- 1 tsp. salt
- ¼ tsp. white pepper, ground
- ⅛ tsp. cayenne pepper, ground
- ⅛ tsp. fresh garlic, minced
- ⅛ tsp. cumin, ground
- ⅛ tsp. fresh sage, finely chopped (optional)
- 1 small bay leaf
- 1 cup heavy whipping cream

Blackened Tuna:

- 6 7-oz. fresh yellowfin tuna steaks, 1½-inches thick
- ¼ cup unsalted butter, melted
- 6 tsps. Chef Paul Prudhomme's Meat Magic Seasoning Smoked Corn Sauce

Smoked Corn Sauce

Melt the butter in a saucepan over medium heat. Add the onions and cook, stirring constantly, until soft and clear. Reduce heat to low and add the corn. Cook the corn, stirring constantly, until very tender, 12 to 15 minutes.

Add all the seasonings and cook for 1 to 2 minutes, stirring constantly and scraping the bottom of the saucepan with a spoon. Add the cream, raise the heat to medium-high and bring the mixture to a boil. Reduce heat to low and simmer for 5 minutes.

* To smoke fresh corn, remove the husks and smoke the whole ears of corn over hickory-wood chips at about 300° for 30 to 40 minutes or until a light brown color is achieved. Do not oversmoke.

Blackened Tuna*

Place the tuna steaks in a shallow pan and season each steak with a light, even amount of meat seasoning, about 1 tsp. each. Add the butter to the pan and coat each steak lightly with butter.

Preheat two 10-inch cast-iron skillets over medium-high heat. (The object in blackening is to quickly sear the tuna, while creating plenty of smoke. The skillets should not be so hot that the butter ignites.)

Let the excess butter drain off, then carefully place 3 tuna steaks into each hot cast-iron skillet. Cook the tuna for about 2 minutes on each side or until medium-rare.

To serve, place 1 tuna steak on each plate and top with ¼ cup of smoked corn sauce and ⅓ cup of red bean salsa.

* Blackening should be done outside or in a kitchen equipped with an adequate exhaust hood and fire extinguishing system.

☆

Smothered Boneless Pork Chops with Lentils

S oak the lentils in water for at least 1 hour before beginning the recipe.

Heat a 2-qt. saucepan over low heat. Add 1 tsp. of the olive oil, ½ cup of carrots, ½ cup of celery and ⅔ cup onion. Cook the vegetables, stirring constantly, until they begin to brown, about 12 to 15 minutes.

Add 1 tsp. of olive oil, garlic, salt and peppers to taste, bay leaf, thyme, oregano and summer savory. Continue cooking, stirring constantly, until the mixture becomes very dark brown and begins sticking to the sides and bottom of the pan, about 5 minutes.

Add the stock or water, turn the heat to high and bring the mixture to a boil.

Add the lentils and return the mixture to a boil. Turn heat to low and let simmer for 10 minutes. Add the remaining 2 Tbsps. each of carrot, celery and onion. Let simmer until the vegetables and lentils are tender, about 5 minutes. Remove from heat.

Season the pork chops lightly with salt and pepper. Heat a 12-inch cast-iron skillet over medium high heat. Add the remaining 2 tsps. of olive oil. When hot, add the pork chops and brown the meat, about 2 minutes on each side. Reduce heat to low and add the lentils and Tabasco Sauce. Simmer uncovered for 15 minutes.

To serve, top each pork chop with the lentil mixture.

Serves 4
Preparation Time:
  45 Minutes
(note soaking time)

- ½ cup lentils
- 4 tsps. olive oil
- ½ cup + 2 Tbsps. carrots, finely diced
- ½ cup + 2 Tbsps. celery, finely diced
- ⅔ cup + 2 Tbsps. onions, finely diced
- 1½ tsps. fresh garlic, minced
- Salt, black and white pepper to taste
- 1 bay leaf
- ⅛ tsp. thyme
- ⅛ tsp. oregano
- ¼ tsp. summer savory
- 3 cups pork, chicken or beef stock or water
- 4 lean boneless pork loin chops, all fat removed, 4 oz. each
- ¼ tsp. Tabasco Sauce

☆

BROUSSARD'S

CONTINENTAL AND CREOLE CUISINE
819 Conti Street
New Orleans, Louisiana
(504) 581-3866
Dinner 5:30 p.m.–10 p.m.
AVERAGE DINNER FOR TWO: $70

Broussard's is one of the Grand Dames of restaurants in New Orleans—a tradition for more than 75 years. Proprietors Gunter and Evelyn Preuss have dedicated their restaurant to perfecting the art of Creole cooking, the most unique indigenous American cuisine.

That means starters such as Crab Meat Ravigote, Shrimp with Two Remoulades and oysters any way you like them, followed by mouthwatering entrees, including Pompano Napoleon, Filet Mignon Josephine and a house specialty, Veal Broussard, and luscious desserts ranging from Bread Pudding with Whiskey Sauce to Bananas Foster.

At Broussard's you will find ambiance and exemplary service equally important in the art of fine dining. Enjoy a New Orleans specialty cocktail—a Sazerac or perhaps a Vin Blanc Cassis—in the peaceful setting of the courtyard with the fragrance of wisteria and night-blooming jasmine.

RECIPE SECRETS FROM BROUSSARD'S

Shrimp and Crab Meat Cheesecake

Crab Meat Broussard's

Pecan Stuffed Salmon

Shrimp and Crab Meat Cheesecake

I n a large bowl, combine the mayonnaise, sour cream, lemon juice, mustard, 3 Tbsps. dill, tarragon, garlic, green onion and paprika. Mix well until everything is incorporated. Fold in the chopped shrimp. Set aside.

Mix the cider vinegar and gelatin in a small skillet and place over medium heat, stirring constantly until gelatin dissolves. Pour the gelatin slowly into the shrimp mixture and mix well. Quickly but gently fold crab meat into mixture and pour into 8-inch springform pan. Cover and refrigerate overnight.

Drain the pimientos and place in a blender with heavy cream, cream cheese and salt. Purée. Pour into a glass bowl and mix in 2 Tbsps. dill. Cover and refrigerate overnight.

To make the pecan mixture, melt the butter in a skillet. Add the pecans, salt, cayenne and Worcestershire. Sauté 2 to 3 minutes but do not burn the mixture. Cool and rough chop. Do not refrigerate.

Remove sides of the springform pan and spread the pimiento sauce over the top of the cheesecake. Take the chopped pecans and press into the sides of the cheesecake. Chill until ready to serve.

Cooking Secret: This dish is not only a great appetizer, but served with a mixed green salad, it makes a perfect lunch entrée.

Serves 6
Preparation Time:
  45 Minutes
(note refrigeration time)

  2 cups mayonnaise
  2 cups sour cream
  4 Tbsps. fresh lemon
    juice
  8 Tbsps. Dijon mustard
  3 Tbsps. fresh dill,
    chopped
  2 tsps. tarragon leaves
  2 tsps. roasted garlic,
    minced
  1 cup green onion, sliced
  2 tsps. paprika
  ¾ lb. cooked shrimp,
    peeled, chopped
 10 Tbsps. cider vinegar
  7½ Tbsps. unflavored
    gelatin
  ¼ lb. crab meat, jumbo
    lump
  1 14 oz. can whole red
    pimientos, about
    2 cups
  ½ cup heavy cream
  8 oz. cream cheese
  1½ tsps. salt
  2 Tbsps. dill
  2 Tbsps. butter
  1 cup pecan pieces
    Salt to taste
    Pinch of cayenne
    pepper
  1 tsp. Worcestershire
    sauce

☆

Crab Meat Broussard's

Serves 6
Preparation Time:
45 Minutes
Preheat oven to 400°

1 Tbsp. butter
6 Jumbo shrimp, peeled,
   butterflied
5 Tbsps. olive oil
1 small onion, diced
2 artichoke hearts,
   chopped
1 garlic clove, minced
¼ cup flour
¼ cup white wine
2 cups chicken stock
1 cup heavy cream
3 oz. Brie cheese
½ cup bread crumbs
1 Tbsp. whole thyme
   leaves
¾ lb. crab meat, jumbo
   lump

I n a large skillet, melt the butter and sauté the shrimp. Set aside to cool.

In a heavy saucepan, heat 2 Tbsps. olive oil and sauté the onion, artichoke and garlic over medium heat until the onion becomes limp. Sprinkle in the flour and mix well. Deglaze with white wine, then add the stock. Reduce the heat and simmer for 3 minutes. Add the heavy cream and simmer another 5 minutes. Remove from heat and let stand 2 to 3 minutes.

Take the Brie and scrape off the white "skin" and cut into small pieces. Add the Brie to the cream sauce and stir until all cheese is melted and mixed well. Let cool.

Mix the bread crumbs, thyme and 3 Tbsps. olive oil. Set aside.

After cheese mixture has cooled, gently fold in the crab meat. Place one shrimp in the center of a 2½ oz. ovenproof dish, so that it stands. If you have a problem, make the butterfly cut deeper. Spoon the crab meat mixture around the shrimp and sprinkle with bread crumb mixture. Repeat with remaining shrimps in remaining dishes.

Place dishes on a cooking pan and place in a 400° oven for 15 to 20 minutes or until hot and bubbly.

☆

Pecan Stuffed Salmon

In a mixing bowl, combine the bread crumbs, pecan pieces, parsley, onion, zest and juice, butter and seasonings. Set aside.

Take the filets and cut a pocket down the middle and into the sides. Stuff the filets with the pecan mixture.

Bake in a 400° oven for about 10 minutes.

Serves 6
Preparation Time:
  20 Minutes
Preheat oven to 400°

- 4 **cups bread crumbs, finely chopped**
- 4 **cups pecan pieces**
- 2 **cups parsley, chopped**
- 2 **cups green onion, thinly sliced**
- ½ **cup lemon zest**
- 1 **cup lemon juice**
- 4 **cups soft butter**
  Cayenne pepper to taste
  Salt and pepper to taste
- 6 **salmon fillets, 6 oz. each**

★

CHARLEY G'S SEAFOOD GRILL

CREOLE-CAJUN
111 Veterans Boulevard.
Metairie, Louisiana 70116
(504) 837-6408
Dinner Nightly 5:30 p.m.–11 p.m.
Lunch Monday–Saturday 11 a.m.–2 p.m.
Brunch Sunday 11 a.m.–1:30 p.m.
AVERAGE DINNER FOR TWO: $80

Between the smart, uncluttered look of the split-level dining space, which is both elegant and festive, and the menu, which contains some of the best Creole-Cajun food around, Charley G's is a runaway success.

The Crab Cakes and Chicken-and-Sausage Gumbo would impress the most discriminating Bayou gastronome. The Game Dishes, especially Duck and Quail, are superb, as are the Grilled Fish and the Final Temptations.

Located on the lobby level of the Heritage Plaza, at the corner of Veterans Boulevard and Lake Avenue, Charley G's treats guests to live Blues during Sunday brunch.

RECIPE SECRETS FROM CHARLEY G'S SEAFOOD GRILL

Polenta Fries

Smoked Duck and Andouille Gumbo

Grilled Asparagus with Strawberry Balsamic Vinaigrette

Smoked, Grilled Soft-Shell Crabs with Citrus Jalapeño Aïoli

White Chocolate Raisinless Bread Pudding with White Chocolate Ganache

Polenta Fries

Bring water to a boil. Add the salt, pepper, garlic and parsley, boiling for 3 minutes. Add the cornmeal in a steady stream, stirring constantly. Continue stirring until the polenta pulls away from the pot edges of the pot about 30 minutes.

Pour out onto a sheet pan. Refrigerate to cool and set.

Cut polenta into large cottage fry batons 1-inch × 4-inch. Fry in hot olive oil until browned and crispy, about 2 minutes.

Sprinkle with kosher salt and serve warm.

Serves 8
Preparation Time:
  25 Minutes
(note refrigeration time)

1¼ qts. water
½ Tbsp. salt
 1 tsp. white pepper
¼ cup garlic, chopped
½ tsp. parsley, chopped
½ lb. coarse cornmeal
   Olive oil for pan frying
½ tsp. kosher salt

Smoked Duck and Andouille Gumbo

Serves 8
Preparation Time:
 30 Minutes
(note simmering time)

 1 smoked duck, 5 lbs.
 1 large onion, diced
 3 stalks celery, diced
 1 medium bell pepper,
   diced
 1 Tbsp. chicken base
 1 Tbsp. beef base
 1 Tbsp. onion,
   granulated
 1 Tbsp. garlic,
   granulated
 1 Tbsp. Creole seasoning
 ½ cup dark roux
 ½ cup blond roux
 2 lbs. andouille sausage,
   diced
   Steamed rice, optional

P eel the meat off the smoked duck. Preserve the meat, discarding the skin, but saving the bones.

Make a duck stock with the smoked bones, half the diced onion, half the diced celery and 1 gallon of water. Simmer for 3 hours, then strain, discarding the bones.

Add the remaining onion, celery, bell pepper, chicken and beef base and the dry seasonings to the smoked duck stock. Bring to a boil.

Add the dark roux and stir until it dissolves. Then add the blond roux at a time until the gumbo comes up to an even consistency.

Dice the smoked duck and add it and the diced andouille to the gumbo. Heat through. Serve with steamed rice on the side.

☆

Grilled Asparagus with Strawberry Balsamic Vinaigrette

Bring a large pot of water to a rolling boil. Blanch asparagus for 45 seconds, then immediately place in ice water to stop the cooking process. Drain well. In a shallow dish, sprinkle asparagus with 1 tsp. kosher salt and 2 tsps. black pepper.

Add the juice of 1 lemon and ½ cup canola oil. Let marinate.

In a food processor or blender, add the strawberries, basil, juice of 2 lemons, honey, balsamic vinegar, 2 tsps. salt and 1 tsp. pepper.

Blend until smooth, and with the machine still running, slowly pour in the oil until all is incorporated. Set aside.

Over a hot grill, cook the marinated asparagus until tender, about 3 to 5 minutes.

Drizzle with vinaigrette. Serve hot or cold.

Serves 4
Preparation Time:
  15 Minutes

> 1 lb. fresh asparagus
> 1 Tbsps. kosher salt
> 1 Tbsp. coarse black pepper
> 3 lemons
> 2½ cups canola oil
> ½ pt. fresh strawberries, stems removed
> 8 fresh basil leaves
> ¼ cup honey
> ¾ cup balsamic vinegar

Smoked, Grilled Soft-Shell Crabs with Citrus Jalapeño Aïoli

Serves 6
Preparation Time:
 1½ Hours
Preheat smoker to 180°

12 large soft-shell crabs
 5 garlic cloves
 1 small fresh jalapeño,
   seeds and stem
   removed
 2 Tbsps. lemon juice
   Salt and white pepper
   to taste
 4 egg yolks
 2 cups olive oil
   Creole seasoning

Cut the crabs across the eyes with kitchen shears or a sharp knife. Reach into the cut and pull out the gray, saclike stomach, called the sand bag. Discard the stomach. Turn the crab over, lift up the flap (sometimes called the apron), and fold it down, away from the body. Gently pull out the apron and attached intestinal vein. Discard the apron and vein. Turn the crabs right side up. Lift flaps at each side near the legs, then scrape off and discard the spongy gills. Crabs are now ready for use.

Gently place the crabs on the smoker, being careful not to break off the legs and claws. Smoke the crabs at 180° for 1 hour using a sweet wood like hickory, cherry or applewood.

Meanwhile, in a food processor, add the garlic, jalapeño, lemon juice, salt and pepper. Purée until smooth. Add the egg yolks. While the machine is running, slowly drizzle in the olive oil until incorporated. The sauce should have a creamy consistency. Adjust salt and pepper to taste.

Brush the crabs with olive oil and sprinkle with Creole seasoning. Place them upside down on a hot, well-oiled grill. Cook for 3 to 4 minutes on each side.

Serve hot with Aïoli for dipping.

Cooking Secret: Serve with your favorite grilled vegetables, such as peppers, eggplant, squash or mushrooms.

White Chocolate Raisinless Bread Pudding with White Chocolate Ganache

In large pot, heat the cream, milk and sugar. Over a double boiler, melt the white chocolate.

Put the eggs and yolks in a large bowl. When the milk mixture is heated, add it to the melted chocolate. Add the chocolate to the eggs. Add the bread and let soak.

Spray a 10-inch pan with oil and line with a parchment circle. Pour bread mixture into the pan and place in a water bath.

Cover with foil and bake at 250° for 45 minutes to 1 hour, or until pudding is set.

Remove the foil and bake 25 to 30 minutes longer, until well set and lightly browned.

Cool and drizzle with White Chocolate Ganache.

White Chocolate Ganache
Heat the cream almost to a boil.

Melt the chocolate over a double boiler. Combine the two slowly, while whisking continuously.

Serves 8
Preparation Time:
  1½ Hours
Preheat oven to 250°

  1 qt. heavy cream
  1 cup milk
  ½ cup sugar
  10 oz. white chocolate
  10 eggs (2 whole, 8 yolks)
  1 to 1½ long loaves stale or toasted French bread, cubed (or enough to soak up mixture)
  Parchment paper to line pan
  White Chocolate Ganache (recipe follows)

White Chocolate Ganache:
  ½ qt. heavy cream
  10 oz. white chocolate

★

COMMANDER'S PALACE

HAUTE CREOLE CUISINE
1403 Washington Avenue
New Orleans, Louisiana 70130
(504) 899-8231
Dinner Daily 6 p.m.–10 p.m.
Lunch Monday–Friday 11:30 a.m.–1:45 p.m.
Brunch Saturday and Sunday 10:30 a.m.–1:30 p.m.
AVERAGE DINNER FOR TWO: $90
Jackets are required for gentlemen at dinner and brunch.

Under Chef Jamie Shannon's direction along with the Brennan family's restaurant experience, Commander's Palace serves as the flagship of a continuing line of award-winning restaurants. Nestled in the middle of New Orleans's Garden District, the Palace stands as a Victorian landmark—complete with turrets, columns and gingerbread accents.

Particular attention is applied to the heart and soul of the restaurant—the kitchen—and the dishes created there. Commander's cuisine reflects the best of the city and both Creole and American heritages, as well as dishes of the restaurant's own creation.

The Palace offers a wide variety of delectable choices for the gastronome, with appetizers such as oven roasted gulf oysters topped with garlic and artichokes and touched with virgin olive oil or the truffle and wild mushroom stew served in a light smoked chicken broth and finished with white truffle oil.

Entree favorites include the roast rack of lamb in a Creole mustard crust and the Lyonnaise Gulf fish served with a potato crust in a caper and onion tomato beurre blanc. Saturdays and Sundays the restaurant hosts a festive jazz brunch with a special menu and live Dixieland band.

RECIPE SECRETS FROM COMMANDER'S PALACE

Shrimp and Tasso with Five-Pepper Jelly

Lyonnaise Fish with Potato Crust

Pecan Pie

Shrimp and Tasso with Five-Pepper Jelly

Make a ¼-inch incision down the back of each shrimp and place one strip of tasso in each incision. Secure with a toothpick. Lightly dust each shrimp with flour and fry. Place the cooked shrimp in a bowl with ½ cup of the Crystal Hot Sauce Beurre Blanc and toss until well coated. Spread Five-Pepper Jelly on the bottom of a small dish and arrange the shrimp on the plate, alternating with the pickled okra.

Crystal Hot Sauce Beurre Blanc

Sauté the garlic and shallot in a pan with a little of the butter. Add the Tabasco Sauce and reduce by ¾. Add the cream and reduce again by half. Slowly stir in the rest of the softened butter, a little at a time.

Five-Pepper Jelly

Place the honey and vinegar in a saucepan and reduce over low heat until sticky. Add the remaining ingredients and cook until the peppers are soft. Season to taste.

Serves 6
Preparation Time:
  30 Minutes

36 jumbo shrimp
   (shelled and deveined)
6 oz. spicy tasso
   (julienned into 1-inch
   strips)
   Flour
   Crystal Hot Sauce
   Beurre Blanc (recipe
   follows)
   Five-Pepper Jelly
   (recipe follows)
36 pickled okra

Crystal Hot Sauce
Beurre Blanc:
   Pinch of garlic
1 shallot, diced
1½ lb. butter, softened
½ cup Tabasco Sauce
¼ cup heavy cream

Five-Pepper Jelly:
⅓ cup honey
¾ cup white vinegar
1 each red, yellow and
   green peppers, diced
1 jalapeño pepper
¼ tsp. black pepper
   Salt to taste

☆

Lyonnaise Fish with Potato Crust

Serves 8
Preparation Time:
30 Minutes

4 lemons
1 tsp. garlic
1 tsp. shallot
1 cup white wine
¼ cup heavy cream
(optional)
1 lb. butter
¼ cup capers
1 tomato peeled, seeded
and diced
1 onion, caramelized
Salt and pepper to
taste
2 eggs
¾ cup milk
8 fresh fillets of fish
(trout, snapper,
sheepshead or catfish)
2 cups flour
6 potatoes, peeled and
sliced, shoestring size
¼ cup oil
Chopped parsley and
chives for garnish

T o make the lemon butter caper sauce, squeeze juice from lemons and add to mashed the pulp in a 2 qt. saucepan. Add garlic, shallot and white wine and simmer until almost dry. Add heavy cream and reduce by ¾ (remember, cream is optional). Add butter, little by little, reducing heat and whisking constantly, being careful not to burn, especially if you have no cream. When all of the butter has been added, remove from heat and strain. Add capers, tomato and caramelized onion. Season to taste.

Prepare the egg wash by mixing the eggs and milk together in a small mixing bowl. Season to taste with salt and pepper and set aside.

Season both sides of fish fillet with salt and pepper. Dust fish in flour. Shake off excess flour, then place in egg wash. Place enough shoestring potato for one side of fish, on a clean, dry surface. Place fish on top of potato and coat top side of fish with potato, forming the potato around the fish.

Place oil in large saucepan over medium-high heat. Cook fish about 3 minutes on each side or until golden brown. (Caramelizing potatoes may prevent sticking).

Serve fish on top of the lemon butter caper sauce and garnish with chopped parsley and chives.

Pecan Pie

Sift flour, salt and sugar into mixing bowl. Cut in butter and shortening with pastry blender or two knives until mixture looks like coarse cornmal. Add water and mix with a fork until dough holds together. Shape into a rough ball and chill for 30 minutes.

Roll out on a floured surface into a circle 2 inches in diameter larger than the pie plate and ⅛-inch thick. Transfer to pan by rolling dough onto rolling pin and unrolling over pan. Ease gently into pan, trim edge and flute. Prick bottom and sides with a fork and bake for 8 to 10 minutes until golden brown. Do not turn oven off.

Meanwhile, cream together the butter and brown sugar. Beat in the eggs, one at a time. Stir in the corn syrup, pecans, vanilla extract and salt.

Fill baked pie shell and decorate top with pecan halves. Bake for 30 minutes in a 375° oven.

Cooking Secret: Dough can be wrapped and refrigerated for several days before using, or it can be frozen.

Yield: 1 pie
Preparation time: 1 Hour
(note chilling time)
Preheat oven to 375°

1¼ cups all-purpose flour
¼ Tbsp. salt
   Dash sugar
8 Tbsps. (1 stick)
   unsalted butter
¼ cup vegetable
   shortening
3 to 4 Tbsps. ice water
⅓ cup butter
¾ cup light brown sugar,
   firmly packed
3 eggs
½ cup light corn syrup
1 cup chopped pecans
1 tsp. vanilla extract
¼ tsp. salt
   Pecan halves for
   garnish

G & E Courtyard Grill

NOUVELLE NEW ORLEANS
1113 Decatur Street
New Orleans, Louisiana 70116
(504) 528-9376
Lunch Friday–Sunday 11:30 a.m.–2:30 p.m.
Dinner Sunday–Saturday 6 p.m.–10 p.m.
AVERAGE DINNER FOR TWO: $80

L ike many French Quarter storefronts, G & E's Decatur Street entrance belies the magical courtyard that is nestled beyond. The quaint, intimate surroundings evoke the feeling of a timeless European café. Watching the rotisserie with delicacies such as whole chickens, duck and fresh salmon cooking, transports you to the most elegant of campfires. The bar choices include a generous selection of fresh squeezed juices and mineral waters, along with the usual list of libations.

Chef/Proprietor Michael Uddo is a young member of a family who not only immortalized the name "G & E" (for grandparents Guiseppe and Elaynora Uddo), but were also instrumental in shaping New Orleans's unique culinary style. Chef Uddo draws on those roots to create a special blend of eclectic flavors.

Cowboy-sized plates offer Louisiana crab cakes paired with homemade goat cheese and gingered black beans or grilled scallops over pasta with smoked Andouille sausage, cream and white beans. The use of fresh, organically grown herbs add a unique twist to his gastronomic wonders.

RECIPE SECRETS FROM G & E COURTYARD GRILL

Oyster Rockefeller Soup

Grilled Louisiana Shrimp with Black Bean-Ginger Vinaigrette, Red Oak Salad

and Fried Tortillas

White Chocolate Bread Pudding with Irish Whiskey Sauce

Oyster Rockefeller Soup

Drain the oysters, reserving the liquid. Purée the oysters in a food processor.

In a large saucepan, over medium heat, combine the puréed oysters, oyster liquid, wine, clam juice, onions and celery. Bring to a light boil and cook over medium heat for 10 minutes.

Whisk in the reduced chicken stock, seafood seasoning and cream and continue whisking until thoroughly blended. Bring to a boil, reduce heat to low and simmer for 10 minutes.

Stir in the spinach and Pernod. Season to taste and serve.

Serves 8
Preparation Time:
** 30 Minutes**

1 qt. oysters
1 bottle dry white wine
2 cups clam juice
2 onions, chopped
5 celery stalks, chopped
3 Tbsps. chicken stock, reduced to a thick glaze
2 to 4 Tbsps. seafood seasoning (recommend Paul Prudhomme's)
1 qt. heavy whipping cream
2 lbs. fresh spinach, cleaned and chopped
Pernod (licorice-flavored liqueur) to taste
Salt and pepper to taste

Grilled Louisiana Shrimp with Black-Ginger Vinaigrette, Red Oak Salad and Fried Tortillas

Serves 6
Preparation Time:
  2½ Hours
(note marinating time)

  1 cup lemon juice
  ½ cup fresh ginger,
    crushed
  2 Tbsps. vegetable oil
  1 Tbsp. garlic, finely
    minced
  2 tsps. Southwestern
    Seasoning (recipe
    follows)
  30 large shrimp
  ¼ tsp. black pepper,
    coarsely ground
  ¼ tsp. ground chili
  ¼ tsp. ground cumin
  ¼ tsp. cayenne pepper
    Salt to taste
  ¼ tsp. oregano
    Black-Ginger Vinai-
    grette (recipe follows)

The Beans:
  ¼ cup black beans, dry
  3 cups water
  1 cup chicken stock
  2 Tbsps. Tabasco Sauce
  ½ large onion, chopped
  3 Tbsps. fresh peeled
    ginger, finely minced
  2 cloves garlic, finely
    minced
  2 bay leaves

In a large bowl, combine lemon juice, ginger, oil, garlic and Southwestern Seasonings for the marinade. Add the shrimp, blend well and marinate in the refrigerator overnight.

Remove the shrimp from the marinade. On a hot grill, a hot skillet or in the broiler, cook the shrimp 2 minutes on each side.

Place the vinaigrette in a saucepan and bring to a boil over medium heat. Add the shrimp to the Black-Ginger Vinaigrette and cook until just done, about 3 minutes.

Place the salad on a large platter and arrange tortillas over the greens. Top with the shrimp and Black-Ginger Vinaigrette and serve soupy.

The Beans
Combine all the ingredients in a pot, cover and soak overnight. On high heat, bring the beans to a boil. Lower the heat and simmer until the beans are tender, about 1½ to 2 hours. Drain and set aside.

Recipe continues on next page.

Black-Ginger Vinaigrette
Combine all the ingredients in a bowl and let sit several hours to allow flavors to blend.

The Salad
Clean and chill the greens.

The Tortillas
Pour one inch of oil into a skillet and heat until almost smoking. Flash-fry the tortillas one at a time until crisp. Remove from the oil and drain on paper towels.

Black-Ginger Vinaigrette:
Preparation Time:
  5 Minutes
(note marinating time)
  1 red pepper, julienned
  1 yellow pepper, julienned
  ½ cup green onion, chopped
  ½ cup pickled Oriental ginger, chopped, with juice
  1 Tbsp. fresh cilantro, chopped
  1 tsp. fresh garlic, finely minced
  ¾ cup red wine vinegar
  1 cup cooked spicy black beans (recipe above)

The Salad:
  1 head radicchio
  2 cups arugula
  1 leek, julienned
  ½ head baby red oak lettuce

The Tortillas:
  6 flour tortillas
    Vegetable oil for frying

☆

White Chocolate Bread Pudding with Irish Whiskey Sauce

Serves 8 to 10
Preparation Time:
  3 Hours
Preheat oven to 400°

  1 loaf day-old French
    bread
  6 eggs
  2 egg yolks
  2 cups milk
  1 cup sugar
  1 cup semi-sweet
    chocolate chips
  ½ cup shaved white
    semi-sweet chocolate
  3 Tbsps. vanilla extract

The Sauce:
  1 whole vanilla bean
  2 cups heavy whipping
    cream
  1 cup Irish whiskey
  ¾ cup granulated sugar
  2 tsps. confectioners'
    sugar
  1 tsp. cornstarch
  3 Tbsps. cold water

S lice the bread and place it in a large mixing bowl. Add all the remaining ingredients and work well until it is thoroughly incorporated. Let stand for 20 minutes. If the mixture becomes dry, add more milk until it is very moist.

Pour the contents of the bowl into a baking dish. Place the dish in a larger roasting pan and carefully add water to the larger pan until it is 1 inch up the sides of the baking dish. Cover the baking dish. Place all in the oven and bake until firm, about 2 to 2½ hours.

The Sauce
Scrape the paste from inside the vanilla bean pod into a saucepan. Add the pod and stir in the cream, whiskey and both the sugars. Place over high heat and bring just to a scald.

Meanwhile, combine the cornstarch and water. Stir the mixture into the saucepan, lower the heat and simmer for 3 minutes. Remove the vanilla bean pod before spooning the sauce over the bread pudding.

☆

GABRIELLE

CONTEMPORARY CREOLE
3201 Esplanade Avenue
New Orleans, Louisiana 70119
(504) 948-6233
Dinner Tuesday–Saturday 5:30 p.m.–10:00 p.m.
Lunch Friday 11:30 a.m.–2:00 p.m. (October through May)
AVERAGE DINNER FOR TWO: $80

Located on Esplanade Avenue, with its dowager mansions and sprawling, ghostly oaks, Gabrielle is a newcomer that has quickly gained top ratings among New Orleans's best. The intimate atmosphere glows with the light of tiny candles, the restaurant is filled with fresh flowers and the dining experience is one of comfortable elegance.

Greg and Mary Sonnier have the background for success. They met while working at K-Paul's. Later, Mary went on to open a catering business, while Greg worked as a sous chef at Brigtsen's. Now they are serving up contemporary Creole cooking in their own restaurant.

The Baked Oysters Gabie, with artichokes and bacon, is a budding classic. The Crawfish Enchilada Con Queso has become too popular to remove from the seasonal menu. Earthy-tasting sausages and imaginative gumbos rival co-chef Mary Sonnier's home-style desserts for undiluted goodness.

With their imaginative Creole-Cajun cooking, the Sonniers have carved a creative niche in the solid foundation of South Louisiana cookery.

RECIPE SECRETS FROM GABRIELLE

Spinach Salad with Pears, Roasted Pecans and Stilton Dressing

Sautéed Red Snapper with Fresh Pepper Vinaigrette

Louisiana Strawberry Shortcake

Spinach Salad with Pears, Roasted Pecans and Stilton Dressing

Serves 6
Preparation Time:
  30 Minutes

  1 **bunch fresh spinach leaves**
  1 **small red onion, thinly sliced**
  1 **fresh pear, thinly sliced (or 1 cup red grapes)**
½ **cup roasted pecans Stilton Dressing (recipe follows)**

Stilton Dressing:
Yield: 6 cups
  2 **egg yolks**
  1 **whole egg**
½ **cup vinegar**
  2 **tsps. fresh lemon juice**
  3 **Tbsps. Creole mustard**
  3 to 4 **cups vegetable oil**
1½ **tsps. kosher salt**
  2 **tsps. white pepper, ground**
  1 **cup crumbled Stilton (or other blue cheese)**
1½ **cups buttermilk**

 oss together fresh spinach, red onion, pear, roasted pecans and dressing.

Stilton Dressing
Mix (or use food processor) together eggs, vinegar, lemon juice and mustard. Gradually add the oil until the mixture is thick. Add seasonings. Add half the cheese and mix well. Stir in the buttermilk and the remaining cheese.

☆

Sautéed Red Snapper with Fresh Pepper Vinaigrette

Heat oil in a 10-inch fry pan until it is about ready to smoke. Season fish, then dredge with flour. Cook the fillets approximately 1 minute on each side, until brown. Remove from pan and drain on paper towels.

Add the stock, onion, tomato and vinegar to the pan. Bring to a boil and whisk in the butter.

Place the fillets on a serving plate and pour the sauce over them.

* Pickled Pepper Vinegar can be made by blending kosher salt and fresh pickled peppers with equal parts of water and apple cider vinegar. Bring mixture to a boil and place in a container. The strength of the mixture depends on the amount and kind of peppers used.

Serves 4
Preparation Time:
  5 Minutes

¼ cup olive oil
2 red snapper fillets,
  8 oz. each
  Seafood seasoning to
  taste
¼ cup flour
⅛ cup seafood stock
¼ cup onion, thinly
  sliced
1 tomato, thinly sliced
⅛ cup Pickled Pepper
  Vinegar*
2 Tbsps. unsalted butter

☆

Louisiana Strawberry Shortcake

Serves 6
Preparation Time:
 45 Minutes
(note refrigeration time)
Preheat oven to 350°

1¼ cups all-purpose flour
 1 cup sugar
 1 Tbsp. baking powder
 ⅛ tsp. salt
 6 Tbsps. cold, unsalted
   butter
 ½ cup cold milk
1½ qts. strawberries,
   washed, hulled and
   sliced
 1 Tbsp. lemon juice
 1 pt. heavy cream
 1 tsp. vanilla extract

Combine the flour, ¼ cup sugar, baking powder and salt in bowl. Mix well. Cut in 5 Tbsps. butter, working with your fingertips until the mixture is coarse (like small peas and not lumpy).

Make a well in the center of the mixture and slowly stir in the cold milk until mixture is thoroughly moistened. Turn mixture onto floured board and knead gently 4 or 5 times.

Roll dough to ¼-inch thickness and cut with 2-inch biscuit cutter. Place cut biscuits on lightly buttered cookie sheet and bake at 350° for 20 minutes or until golden brown. Cool.

Mix sliced strawberries with lemon juice and ½ cup sugar or to taste. Cover and let stand in the refrigerator for about 1 hour before serving.

Whip cream slightly, adding ¼ cup sugar and the vanilla. Continue to whip until soft peaks form. Do not overwhip.

Split biscuits in half with fork. Butter both halves with the remaining 1 Tbsp. butter and toast in the oven.

Place biscuits, toasted side up, on serving dish. Spoon on strawberry mixture. Place other half of biscuit over strawberry mixture, also toasted side up. Add additional strawberry mixture and top with whipped cream.

☆

GALATOIRE'S

FRENCH-CREOLE CUISINE
209 Bourbon Street
New Orleans, Louisiana
(504) 525-2021
Lunch and Dinner Daily 11:30 a.m.–9 p.m.
AVERAGE DINNER FOR TWO: $70

Trendy places come and go, but certain traditions endure in New Orleans. For Friday lunch, Galatoire's is the place. It's the place to see and be seen and, of course, to eat. There is a sense of excitement and *joie de vivre* at Galatoire's. Diners often say it feels like Mardi Gras. It's a party in the splendor of one of the city's landmarks.

Family-owned and operated since 1905, Galatoire's prides itself on the fact that its traditions remain constant throughout the eras. With mirrored walls, white tile floors, chandeliers and brass fixtures, it is one of the prettiest restaurants in New Orleans. The service is impeccable—waiters serve you in tuxedos!

Galatoire's specialties include Shrimp Rémoulade, Chicken Clemenceau, Sirloin Marchand de Vin, Broccoli Hollandaise and Crêpes Maison. The menu also includes Crab Meat Cocktails, Stuffed Avocado with Crabmeat Salad, Stuffed Tomato with Shrimp Salad, a Portobello Mushroom Platter, Rockefeller Spinach, Cherries Jubilee, Crêpes Suzette and a wonderful Chocolate Nut Sundae.

RECIPE SECRETS FROM GALATOIRE'S

Crab Meat Maison

Oysters en Brochette

Trout Meunière Amandine

Crab Meat Maison

Serves 6
Preparation Time:
** 30 Minutes**

½ cup homemade
   mayonnaise
3 Tbsps. French dressing
   (olive oil, vinegar,
   Creole mustard, salt
   and pepper to taste)
3 green onions, finely
   chopped
1 tsp. capers
½ tsp. parsley, chopped
1 lb. crab meat
12 lettuce slices
12 tomato slices
   Juice from 1 lemon

Mix mayonnaise, French dressing, onions, capers, and parsley together. Once thoroughly mixed, fold in the crab meat. Serve over a bed of lettuce with two slices of tomato on the sides. Squeeze lemon juice over salad just before serving.

☆

Oysters en Brochette

F ry bacon until not quite crisp. Alternate 6 oysters and 6 half strips of bacon (folded) on each skewer. Beat together egg and milk and seasoning well with salt and pepper. Dip each skewer in egg and milk mixture, roll in flour and deep fry until golden. Serve on toast with lemon wedges.

Serves 4
Preparation Time:
  15 Minutes

 12 bacon strips, cut in
     half
  2 dozen raw oysters
  4 skewers, 8-inches each
  1 egg
 ¾ cup milk
     Salt and pepper to
     taste
  2 cups flour
     Oil for deep frying
  4 bread slices, toasted
  2 lemons, cut in wedges,
     garnish

☆

Trout Meunière Amandine

Serves 4
Preparation Time:
  30 Minutes

  4 speckled trout fillets,
    6 to 8 oz. each
    Salt and pepper to
    taste
  1 cup milk
  1 cup flour
    Oil for frying
  ½ lb. butter
  4 oz. almonds, sliced,
    toasted
    Juice of 1 lemon
  ½ Tbsp. parsley, chopped,
    garnish

alt and pepper trout fillets and dip in milk, then roll in flour. Fry in hot oil in a shallow pan until golden on both sides.

In a separate pan, melt and continuously whip butter until brown and frothy. Add almonds and lemon juice. Pour over trout. Garnish with parsley.

GAUTREAU'S

CONTINENTAL
1728 Soniat Street
New Orleans, Louisiana 70115
(504) 899-7397
Dinner Monday–Saturday 6 p.m.–10 p.m.
Lunch Monday–Friday 11:30 a.m.–2 p.m.
AVERAGE DINNER FOR TWO: $80

T his cozy uptown neighborhood dining room with French bistro overtones was originally a pharmacy. The antique apothecary showcases now display wine and liquor selections, the walls exhibit archival photographs and the ceiling is paneled in the original embossed tin.

Gautreau's, an award-winning restaurant, serves continental cuisine with strong Mediterranean and Asian influences. Selections range from Tamari Glazed Muscovy Duck Breasts or Curried Vegetables with Sticky Rice to Tournedos of Black Angus Beef. Japanese Noodles are paired with Grilled Shrimp, Oranges and Fresh Cilantro. Fresh Crawfish is infused with Tarragon and served over a Lemony Couscous with Grapes. Expect a menu change every six weeks to make use of fresh, seasonal ingredients.

RECIPE SECRETS FROM GAUTREAU'S

Cream of Corn Soup with Lump Crab Meat

Roasted Lamb Loin with Celery-Root Mashed Potatoes, Ratatouille and Lavender Lamb Jus

Tequila Key Lime Pie

Cream of Corn Soup

Serves 4
Preparation Time:
   30 Minutes

8 Tbsps. (1 stick) butter
1 yellow onion, diced
5 stalks celery, diced
2 cups fresh white or
   yellow corn, shaved off
   the cob
   Flour
1 cup fish stock or light
   chicken stock
1½ qts. cream
½ tsp. thyme, dried
5 bay leaves
½ tsp. cayenne pepper
2 Tbsps. bourbon
½ cup lump crab meat
   (shells removed)
   Salt and white pepper
   to taste
   Chopped parsley for
   garnish

In a heavy pot, melt the butter over low heat.
Add the onion and celery, stirring constantly. When onion is translucent, add the corn and continue to cook and stir until the corn is tender.

Add enough flour to coat all the vegetables; stir in well.

Add the stock slowly while stirring, until all is incorporated. Stir in the cream, thyme, bay leaves and cayenne. Simmer for 20 minutes.

Add the bourbon and remove from heat.

Heat up the crab meat in a small amount of butter. Place the heated crab meat in the bottom of the serving bowls. Pour the soup over the crab meat. Season to taste and garnish with parsley.

Roasted Lamb Loin with Celery-Root Mashed Potatoes, Ratatouille and Lavender Lamb Jus

Heat oil in a large sauté pan over high heat. Season the lamb with salt and pepper and sear on both sides. Place in preheated 400° oven and cook for 7 minutes. While the lamb is cooking, strain the fat from the sauté pan. Place back over medium heat and add the shallots and sauté for 30 seconds. Add the red wine, scraping the lamb bits from the bottom of the pan. Reduce the wine to 1 Tbsp.

Add the stock and lavender. Reduce by half.

Swirl in the butter before serving and simmer for 1 minute. Adjust seasonings to taste.

To serve, place a small amount of potatoes in the center of each serving plate. Slice and fan the lamb around the potatoes. Add the ratatouille in the center of the lamb and on top of the potatoes and add the sauce around the lamb.

Serves 2
Preparation Time:
  25 Minutes
Preheat oven to 400°

Roasted Lamb Loin with Lavender:
  1 **Tbsp. canola oil**
  2 **lamb loins, silver skin removed**
    Salt and pepper to taste
  4 **shallots, chopped**
  1 **cup red wine**
  2 **cups lamb or veal stock**
  1 **Tbsp. lavender**
  2 **Tbsps. butter**
    Celery-Root Mashed Potatoes (recipe follows on next page)
    Ratatouille (recipe follows, page 195)

☆

Celery-Root Mashed Potatoes

Serves 2
Preparation Time:
25 Minutes

2 Idaho potatoes, peeled
  and cut into quarters
2 medium-sized bulbs of
  celery root, cut into
  quarters
  Butter as needed
  Warm cream as
  needed
  Salt and white pepper
  to taste
½ tsp. celery seeds

Boil the potatoes in salted water for 7 to 8 minutes. Add the celery root and continue to boil until tender.

Ratatouille

Heat a large pot over medium heat. Add the olive oil and stir in the pepper, squash, zucchini, onion and mushrooms. When the mixture begins to sweat out its moisture, add the eggplant, tomatoes, garlic and dry herbs.

Constantly stir over medium to low heat until all the flavors have blended and the vegetables are slightly mushy.

Season with salt and pepper. If the ratatouille looks dry, add some tomato juice.

Serves 2
Preparation Time:
** 30 Minutes**

1 Tbsp. olive oil
1 red bell pepper, seeded and diced
1 yellow squash, diced
1 zucchini, diced
1 small yellow onion, diced
1 cup fresh mushrooms
1 small eggplant, peeled and diced
2 tomatoes, peeled, seeded and diced
1 tsp. garlic, chopped
½ tsp. dry thyme
½ tsp. dry oregano
2 bay leaves
  Salt and pepper to taste

☆

Tequila Key Lime Pie

Yield: 1 pie
Preparation Time:
  20 Minutes
(note refrigeration time)

10 egg yolks
 1 cup sugar
½ cup lime juice
½ cup tequila
    Zest of 1 lime
½ lb. butter, cubed, cold
    10-inch pie shell,
    prebaked

Cook the yolks, sugar, lime juice, tequila and lime zest by slowly stirring in a double boiler over water for 10 to 15 minutes. When mixture is thick, remove from the heat and add in the cold, cubed butter.

Pour into prebaked pie shell and refrigerate for 2 hours.

☆

KELSEY'S RESTAURANT

CAJUN
3823 Magazine Street
New Orleans, Louisiana 70115
(504) 897-6722
Lunch Tuesday–Friday 11 a.m.–2:00 p.m.
Dinner Tuesday–Saturday 5:30 p.m.–9:30 p.m.
AVERAGE DINNER FOR TWO: $85

F rom Kelsey's kitchen pours a rich bounty of fabulous food, bursting with the earthy vigor of the South Louisiana culinary tradition. The flavors never lose their balance or resort to blasts of searing seasonings to make an impression. The guiding genius at Kelsey's is Chef Randy Barlow, a native, who made his way into the kitchens of the early Cajun masters. Chef Barlow has emerged with a unique repertoire of tastes, which quickly gained recognition when he and his wife opened Kelsey's.

The menu displays a willingness to look beyond Louisiana for flavors, in a superb blending of ethnic variations offering tempting creations such as a starter of pastry filled with shrimp, drizzled with a curry sauce or a superb grilled salmon topped with shrimp and lavished with a vibrant roasted red pepper and cilantro mousseline. His panéed rabbit comes shrouded in a breading both flaky and substantial, served with a velvety cream sauce and fettuccine infused with just the right amount of smoky tasso. At Kelsey's, you can count on generous portions and gumbo specials every day.

RECIPE SECRETS FROM KELSEY'S

Eggplant and Tomato Soup with Bacon and Sour Cream

Pasta Kelsey

Apple-Raspberry Crisp

Eggplant and Tomato Soup with Bacon and Sour Cream

Serves 4
Preparation Time:
  45 Minutes

  8 **Tbsps. (1 stick) of**
    butter
  1 **cup flour**
 12 **slices bacon, diced**
  1 **cup onions, diced**
  ½ **cup bell peppers, diced**
  ½ **cup celery, diced**
  2 **medium eggplants,**
    peeled and diced
  ½ **tsp. dried basil**
  ½ **tsp. dried oregano**
    Salt and pepper to
    taste
  1 **14-oz. can tomatoes,**
    cut (reserve juice)
  4 **cups chicken stock**
  1 **tsp. brown sugar**
  1 **cup heavy cream**
  1 **cup sour cream**
  1 **Tbsp. curry powder**

T o make a blond roux, melt the butter over medium heat and add the flour slowly. Stir until the consistency is a creamy paste. Set aside.

Brown the bacon. Add the onions, peppers and celery and cook until translucent over medium-high heat, about 5 minutes.

Add the eggplant and cook for 5 more minutes, stirring often.

Add the basil, oregano, salt and pepper.

Stir in the tomatoes and their juice and bring to a boil.

Add the stock and the brown sugar. Cook for 15 minutes.

Thicken with the prepared roux, adding only small amounts at a time while the soup continues to boil.

Add the cream and sour cream and cook for an additional 10 minutes. Add the curry powder and adjust seasonings to taste.

☆

Pasta Kelsey

Heat oil in a large skillet over medium-high heat. Add the herbs and garlic.

Add the shrimp and fish and cook until the shrimp turns pink, about 1 minute.

Add the oysters, green onions, tomato and stock. Bring to a boil. Immediately add the Worcestershire sauce and lemon juice.

Add the crab meat. Do not overcook seafood. Season with salt and peppers to taste.

Add the butter, stirring to incorporate. Add both cheeses. Serve over pasta.

Cooking Secret: "Eggplant Kelsey" is a delicious dish using eggplant instead of pasta. Use two eggplant rounds per serving. Dust ¼-inch-thick peeled eggplant rounds in flour. Place in an egg wash (an egg and milk mixture). Drain and cover with bread crumbs (may use seasoned bread crumbs). Fry in heated olive oil over medium heat 3 minutes on each side or until golden brown. Drain. Spoon sauce over eggplant rounds.

Serves 4
Preparation Time:
 30 Minutes

  2 **Tbsps. olive oil**
 ½ **tsp. fresh basil, minced**
 ½ **tsp. fresh oregano, minced**
 ½ **tsp. fresh parsley, minced**
 ½ **tsp. garlic, minced**
 20 **to 24 shrimp**
  1 **cup diced fish, any variety**
 24 **oysters (approximately 1 cup)**
  1 **bunch green onions, chopped**
  1 **tomato, diced**
 1½ **cups seafood stock, fresh or canned**
  1 **tsp. Worcestershire sauce**
  1 **Tbsp. lemon juice**
 ½ **cup crab meat**
    Salt, red and black pepper to taste
  8 **Tbsps. (1 stick) unsalted butter**
  2 **Tbsps. Parmesan cheese**
  2 **Tbsps. Romano cheese Angel hair pasta, cooked al dente**

★

Apple-Raspberry Crisp

Yield: 1 10-inch cake
Preparation Time:
 45 Minutes
Preheat oven to 350°

 4 **Golden Delicious or**
   Granny Smith apples,
   peeled, cored and
   diced (about 2 cups)
 1 **cup fresh or frozen**
   raspberries
1½ **cups sugar**
 8 **Tbsps. (1 stick) butter,**
   room temperature
 1 **stick margarine, room**
   temperature
 1 **cup all-purpose flour**
   Ice cream or whipped
   cream, optional

I n a medium bowl, mix together the apples raspberries, and ½ cup sugar.

Spread evenly in a greased 10-inch cake pan.

In a medium bowl, knead together the butter, margarine, remaining cup sugar and flour until crumbly.

Sprinkle over the fruit. Bake at 350° for 30 minutes or until golden brown. Serve plain or with ice cream or whipped cream.

☆

LA MADELEINE

FRENCH COUNTRY, with a hint of Indochine
601 South Carrollton Avenue.
New Orleans, Louisiana 70118
(504) 861-8661
Breakfast and Lunch daily 7a.m.–closing
Dinner Sunday–Saturday 5 p.m.–10 p.m.
AVERAGE DINNER FOR TWO: $25

Ginger, soy, cumin, coriander and banana in French country cooking? Quelle surprise! La Madeleine's ingenious chefs have infused traditional, hearty, fresh French fare with fresh new herbs, seasonings and surprising flavor blends. The result is menu creations as exotic as an Asian orchid.

According to Executive Chef and Frenchman Remy Schaal, Southeast Asian influences have been a part of French cooking since as early as the 1700s. But make no mistake; this food is such authentic, hearty French country that you can taste the accent.

La Madeleine responds to seasonal changes by rotating menu items and developing new dishes according to guest preferences. Menu highlights include Carrot and Ginger Cream Soup, Stuffed Sweet Peppers Filled with Vegetables in a Savory Mixture and Seafood Cocotte; a medley of Scallops, Tilapia and Crawfish in a Spicy Poblano Pepper Sauce. Gourmet sandwiches, made in the traditional French manner, with the special paniné rolls, are served warm and stuffed to the brim with tasty fillings and fresh vegetables. Save room for the Caramel and Roasted Pecan Cheesecake. Straight from the pâtisserie, this grand finale is la Madeleine's latest naughty little dessert. Alongside the aromatic spices, guests will find a warm, inviting ambiance and outstanding service—*joie de servir.*

RECIPE SECRETS FROM LA MADELEINE'S

Carrot and Ginger Cream Soup

Stuffed Sweet Peppers

Rotisserie Turkey

Carrot And Ginger Cream Soup

Serves 6
Preparation time:
  30 Minutes

  2 lbs. carrots
  ¼ stick unsalted butter
  **1 Tbsp. ginger, freshly
    grated**
  **2 cloves garlic, finely
    chopped**
  **½ Anaheim chile, finely
    chopped (mild green
    chile)**
3½ cups water
  **1 vegetable bouillon
    cube**
  ½ tsp. salt
  ¼ tsp. ground coriander
  ¾ cup light table cream

Peel carrots and slice into chunks and set aside. Set aside 2 carrots and dice into little cubes for later use.

In medium-sized saucepan, melt butter over medium heat and add the ginger, garlic and chile. Cook for 30 seconds, being careful not to brown the mixture. Add the water and carrot chunks and bring to a boil.

Add the vegetable bouillon cube, salt and coriander. Cook over medium heat for approximately 20 minutes or until the carrots are soft.

Pour the carrot soup into a blender and process until puréed. Return puréed soup to pan and bring to a boil, stirring occasionally.

Add the cream and the remaining cubed carrots and bring to a slow boil for 5 minutes.

Adjust the seasonings to taste and serve piping hot or chilled.

Stuffed Sweet Peppers

C ut the red peppers in half, removing the core and seeds, and set aside.

In a mixing bowl combine the sliced green peppers, red onions, zucchini, yellow squash, garlic and olive oil and toss thoroughly. Place the vegetable mixture on a cookie sheet and grill at 400° for approximately 15 minutes or until golden brown. Allow to cool.

In a separate bowl, mix the cooked rice, diced tomatoes, fresh basil, cilantro, Parmesan cheese, salt, coriander and cumin. Add the grilled vegetables and mix well.

Fill each red pepper with the mixture and cover with foil. Place in the oven and cook for 45 minutes.

Serves 4
Preparation Time:
  1 Hour
Preheat oven to 400°

  4 red peppers
  ¾ cup green peppers, sliced
  ¾ cup red onions, sliced
  ¾ cup zucchini, sliced
  ¾ cup yellow squash, sliced
  5 garlic cloves, crushed
  2 Tbsps. extra virgin olive oil
  2 cups wild rice, cooked
  4 medium tomatoes, diced
  8 basil leaves, finely chopped
 10 sprigs cilantro, finely chopped
  ¼ cup grated Parmesan cheese
  ½ tsp. salt
  ¼ tsp. ground coriander
  ⅛ tsp. ground cumin

Rotisserie Turkey

Serves 8
Preparation Time:
  1½ Hours
Preheat oven to 375°

  1 tsp. paprika
  2 tsps. garlic, granulated
  2 tsps. salt
  ½ tsp. black pepper,
    cracked
    Chopped rind of
    ½ lemon
  1 **turkey breast, whole,**
    boned, skin-on

I n a bowl, mix together all the spices and lemon rind and spread evenly around the turkey breast.
Place the turkey in the preheated oven for 20 minutes. Reduce the oven temperature to 325° and allow to cook for another hour or until the internal temperature is 165°.

Remove from oven when the turkey breast is cooked through and tender.

Cooking Secret: The turkey breast, infused with the fresh blend of spices, can be enhanced with Pomery mustard or mushroom sauce when serving.

★

LA PROVENCE

FRENCH
Four miles west on U.S. 190
Lacombe, Louisiana 70445
(504) 626-7662
Dinner Wednesday–Saturday 5 p.m.–11 p.m.
Dinner Sunday 1 p.m.–9 p.m.
AVERAGE DINNER FOR TWO: $85

Although La Provence is almost an hour's drive from New Orleans, the glorious French Provincial food and relaxing atmosphere of this exceptional restaurant are well worth the trip. For more than two decades, La Provence Restaurant has been ranked among New Orleans' ten best on virtually every listing.

Award-winning chef-owner Chris Kerageorgiou's elegant yet earthy cooking is consistently satisfying. His love affair with food has ripened into a wonderful marriage, uniting the best of his classic French training with fresh local ingredients. Here in his impressive kitchen he produces pleasures for the palette that prompted praise in Charles Kuralt's "America": "The sauces alone make La Provence one of the best restaurants in the world."

Giant New Zealand Mussels, still in their shells under a Garlicky Butter Sauce, arrive on Angel Hair Pasta; Tenderloin of Rabbit is swathed in a light gravy redolent of lavender; Roasted Duck with Garlic warms the soul; and a thick and hearty Quail Gumbo with Rice and Andouille Sausage is a revelation.

Separating the two dining rooms, hung with pleasant Provençal landscape paintings, is a hearth that welcomes you on damp winter days. The congenial, tree-shaded deck is open during warmer seasons.

RECIPE SECRETS FROM LA PROVENCE

Soupe de Poisson

Ratatouille

Chicken with Garlic, Olives and Tomatoes

Soupe de Poisson

Serves 10
Preparation Time:
  30 Minutes

  2 lbs. white fish, diced
    Salt and pepper to
    taste
  ¼ cup olive oil
  ½ cup leek, chopped
  ½ cup fennel, chopped
  1 large onion, chopped
  4 cloves garlic, minced
  2 large potatoes, diced
  1 tsp. lemon juice
  ½ cup white wine
  1 tsp. saffron
  ½ gal. fish stock
  2 whole bay leaves
  2 sprigs thyme
    Red pepper flakes to
    taste
  ¼ cup Ricard (anise-
    flavored liqueur),
    optional

S eason the fish with salt and pepper.
      In a large sauté pan, cook the fish in the olive oil over moderate heat with the leek, fennel, onion, garlic and potatoes for 5 minutes.

Add the lemon juice, white wine and saffron and cook for 5 minutes more. Add the fish stock, bay leaves, thyme and red pepper flakes and cook for 20 minutes.

Remove from heat and purée in a food mill or food processor. Adjust the seasonings to taste and add the Ricard, if desired.

Cooking Secret: Serve hot, topped with Gruyere cheese, or add pasta. Chef Chris suggests pairing with a Chateau Roubine white wine.

Ratatouille

Cut the eggplants in half lengthwise, then score them lengthwise down the cut side, being careful not to cut through the skin. Brush a baking sheet with about ½ tsp. olive oil and place the eggplant on it, cut side down. Bake for 15 to 20 minutes, until the skins begin to shrivel. Remove from the heat and allow to cool. When cool enough to handle, cut into ½- to 1-inch cubes. If you wish, you can peel the eggplant before dicing.

Turn the oven down to 350°. Brush the inside of a lidded earthenware casserole dish with ½ tsp. olive oil.

Heat 1 Tbsp. of the olive oil in a heavy-bottomed, nonstick skillet over medium heat and add the onions. Cook, stirring, until they begin to soften, about 5 minutes. Add 2 of the sliced garlic cloves and cook, stirring, for another 4 or 5 minutes. Transfer to the casserole.

Heat the remaining Tbsp. of olive oil in the skillet and add the peppers. After a couple of minutes, season with salt and continue to cook, stirring, until the peppers begin to soften. Add the zucchini and 2 more sliced garlic cloves and cook with the peppers for 5 minutes or until the zucchini begins to look a little translucent. Transfer to the casserole with the onions. Add the diced eggplant and half the tomatoes to the casserole, along with the tomato paste, bay leaf, thyme and about 1 tsp. salt. Toss well and bake for 1½ hours.

After the first 30 minutes, give the stew a good stir and add the remaining tomatoes and the whole garlic cloves. Adjust the seasonings and bake for the last 30 minutes. Stir in the basil, cover, and return to the oven. Turn off the heat and leave the ratatouille in the oven for another hour.

Place a colander over a bowl and drain the juices off the ratatouille. Transfer the juices to a saucepan and bring to a boil. Reduce by half. Return the ratatouille to the earthenware dish and stir in the juices. Taste and adjust seasonings. Serve hot or cold.

Cooking Secret: Ratatouille is best made a day ahead of time and will keep 4 to 5 days in the refrigerator. It can be frozen.

Serves 6
Preparation Time:
3 Hours
Preheat oven to 475°

- 2 large eggplants
- 2 Tbsps. + 1 tsp. olive oil
- 2 large onions, sliced
- 6 large garlic cloves, sliced (leave 2 whole)
- 1 large red bell pepper, sliced into 1×2-inch strips
- 1 large green bell pepper, sliced into 1×2-inch strips
- Salt to taste
- 3 zucchini halved and sliced ½-inch thick
- 4 tomatoes, peeled, seeded and coarsely chopped
- 1 Tbsp. tomato paste
- 1 bay leaf
- 2 tsps. fresh thyme leaves
- Pepper, freshly ground to taste
- 1 tsp. salt
- Fresh basil to taste

Chicken with Garlic, Olives and Tomatoes

Serves 6
Preparation Time:
  45 Minutes

  1 chicken, quartered,
    about 3 lbs.
    Salt and freshly
    ground pepper to taste
  2 Tbsps. olive oil
  1 onion, thinly sliced
 10 garlic cloves, coarsely
    chopped
  1 lb. tomatoes, peeled,
    seeded and chopped
  2 Tbsps. fresh thyme
    leaves
  1 bay leaf
  1 cup white wine
  1 cup chicken stock or
    canned broth
 ¼ cup black oil-cured
    olives, pitted
  2 Tbsps. fresh parsley
    Rice or pasta, cooked
    Olives for garnish
    Parsley for garnish

S eason chicken with salt and pepper. Heat the olive oil in a large nonstick skillet over high heat and brown the chicken.

Add the onion and garlic and cook for several minutes or until the onion has become translucent.

Add the tomatoes, thyme and bay leaf. Continue cooking over medium heat for 1 minute, then add the wine and reduce the liquid by half.

Add the chicken stock and simmer for 10 minutes. Salt and pepper to taste.

Just before serving, reheat and serve over pasta or rice. Garnish with olives and parsley.

La Riviera

ITALIAN CUISINE
4506 Shores Drive
Metairie, Louisiana 70006
(504) 888-6238
Lunch Tuesday–Friday 11:30 a.m.–2 p.m.
Dinner Monday–Saturday 5:30 p.m.–10 p.m.
AVERAGE DINNER FOR TWO: $85

For more than twenty years the combined talents of Chef Goffredo Fraccaro and Proprietor Valentino Rovere have delighted a loyal and devoted following. La Riviera was born in Metairie and soon was anchored securely with the top restaurants in the city. Homemade pastas, innovative sauces and boldly imaginative preparations earned recognition and honors in the industry.

Chef Fraccaro came to New Orleans from Italy, bringing with him a pioneering spirit and many special dishes. Today, he offers traditional Northern Italian cuisine at La Riviera, where the seafood is fresh, the pasta is homemade and the service is friendly.

The decor's inspiration covers several centuries, from Renaissance to Rococo, to late 20th century rudimentary, in a large, comfortable dining room.

Specialties include Cannelloni, Veal (nine splendid variations) and the award-winning Crab Meat Ravioli in a sauce of Cream and Parmesan. The desserts, which are works of art, are made fresh on the premises. The cappuccino (one of the best in town) guarantees an encore.

RECIPE SECRETS FROM LA RIVIERA

Crab Meat Ravioli

Crawfish Spaghetti

Scampi Genovese

Veal Shanks with Mushrooms

Tiramisù

Crab Meat Ravioli

Serves 6
Preparation Time:
 30 Minutes
(note refrigeration time)

Crab Meat Filling:
 1½ **cups heavy cream**
   Salt and pepper to
   taste
   5 **Tbsps. butter, softened**
   1 **lb. lump crab meat,**
   picked over for bits of
   shell
 ¼ **cup green onion,**
   minced
 ½ **cup cracker crumbs**
   Salt and white pepper
   to taste
   Parsley for garnish
 ¼ **cup freshly grated**
   Parmesan cheese

Ravioli Dough:
 ½ **cup flour**
   1 **egg, slightly beaten**
   1 **Tbsp. water**
   1 **Tbsp. oil or clarified**
   butter

Ravioli Sauce:
   1 **cup whipping cream,**
   reduced by half
 ¼ **cup butter**
   Salt, red and white
   pepper to taste

For the filling: in a heavy saucepan, reduce the cream by ⅓ and season with salt and pepper. Whisk in 4 Tbsps. butter. Add the picked crab meat to the sauce.

Melt 1 Tbsp. butter in a pan and sauté the onions until they are clear but not browned. Add the onions and cracker crumbs to the cream sauce and mix to combine. Refrigerate to cool while you prepare the dough for the ravioli.

Ravioli Dough
Put the flour in a large bowl and add the egg, 1 Tbsp. water and 1 Tbsp. oil or clarified butter. Work with your hands or a wooden spoon until thoroughly mixed and dough forms into a ball. Knead for 5 to 6 minutes. Set in a bowl to rest for about 1 hour.

On a floured board or other smooth surface, roll the dough paper thin. You will need 2 sheets to form the ravioli. Shape the crab meat filling into balls the size of large marbles. Place them about 1½-inches apart on 1 sheet of the pasta dough. Paint the area between the balls with water and top with the second sheet of dough. Form the ravioli by pressing around each ball to form a seal. Dust with flour and cut into squares. Cook for 5 minutes in rapidly boiling, salted water. Drain.

Ravioli Sauce
Cook the reduced whipping cream, butter and seasonings until slightly boiling. Drizzle the sauce over the ravioli and sprinkle with parsley. Top with the grated Parmesan cheese.

Crawfish Spaghetti

Make the white sauce by melting 4 Tbsps. (or ¼ cup) butter over low heat in a 2-qt. saucepan. Stir in the flour, salt and pepper. Remove the white sauce from the heat.

Bring the milk just to a boil and pour into the butter-flour mixture. Place over high heat, stirring constantly until it bubbles. Set aside.

In a 3-qt. saucepan, melt the remaining butter. Sauté the red pepper, garlic, onions, parsley and tomatoes. Simmer over medium heat for 5 minutes. Add half of the white sauce, stirring thoroughly.

Add the crawfish tails. Adjust the seasonings to taste.

Add the rest of the white sauce and serve over freshly cooked pasta.

Serves 4
Preparation Time:
 30 Minutes

 8 oz. (1 cup or 2 sticks) butter or margarine
½ cup flour
¼ tsp. salt and pepper
 1 qt. milk
¼ tsp. red pepper, crushed
¼ tsp. garlic, minced
 3 bunches green onion, chopped
 2 tsps. parsley, chopped
 1 cup tomatoes, chopped
 1 to 2 lbs. crawfish tails, cooked
 1 lb. pasta, cooked

Scampi Genovese

Serves 4
Preparation Time:
 30 Minutes
Preheat oven to 375°

 2 cloves garlic, chopped
 ¼ cup parsley, chopped
 ¼ tsp. oregano
 4 Tbsps. olive oil
 1 tsp. balsamic vinegar
 2 Tbsps. fresh mint
   leaves
 2 lbs. jumbo shrimp, raw
   Salt and pepper
 1 Tbsp. paprika
 ½ stick butter, melted
 3 Tbsps. lemon juice
 1 lb. angel hair pasta or
   rice, cooked
 6 lemon wedges for
   garnish

I n a mixing bowl, blend the garlic, parsley, oregano, olive oil, balsamic vinegar and mint. Set aside.

Remove the shells from the shrimp, leaving the tails on. Devein and wash shrimp under cold water. Dry with a towel.

Coat a baking pan with olive oil. Arrange the shrimp in a single layer, adding salt and pepper to taste and the paprika.

Bake in the preheated oven for 10 minutes.

Remove from the oven and combine shrimp, sauce, butter and lemon juice in an ovenproof dish or pot. Return to the oven for 3 minutes or until the butter is melted. Up to 2 Tbsps. of water may be added if it becomes to dry.

Serve this dish as a main course with angel hair pasta or rice, garnished with lemon wedges.

☆

Veal Shanks with Mushrooms

Brown the onion, carrot, celery, garlic and parsley in the oil in a stovetop casserole dish over medium heat. Dredge the veal shanks in the flour and add them to the vegetables. Brown evenly. Season with salt and pepper and add the wine.

When the wine has partially evaporated, add the tomato purée and stock, pouring it over the meat. Bring to a boil and reduce the heat.

Add the rosemary. Cover and simmer slowly for 1½ to 2 hours.

Add the mushrooms and simmer a few minutes longer before serving.

Serves 6
Preparation Time:
  2½ Hours

  1 **onion, finely chopped**
  1 **carrot, finely chopped**
  1 **celery stalk, finely**
     chopped
  2 **cloves garlic, chopped**
  2 **Tbsps. parsley,**
     chopped
 ½ **cup olive oil**
  6 **veal shanks, about**
     ½ lb. each
 ½ **cup flour**
     Salt and pepper
 ¾ **cup white wine**
  2 **cups tomato purée**
  2 **Tbsps. clear stock**
  1 **tsp. rosemary**
 ½ **lb. mushrooms**

Tiramisù

Serves 12
Preparation Time:
  45 Minutes
(note refrigeration time)

1½ pts. whipping cream
  1 Tbsp. unflavored
    gelatin powder
  6 eggs, separated (room
    temperature)
2½ cups sugar, divided
  2 packages cream
    cheese, 8 oz. each
    (room temperature)
  ½ cup espresso or strong
    coffee
  2 Tbsps. brandy
  1 package lady finger
    cookies (approx. 1 lb.)
  ¼ cup cocoa powder

Warm ½ cup cream in a saucepan over low heat. Blend in the gelatin. Set aside to cool.

Beat 6 egg whites with ¼ cup sugar and set aside. Whip remaining cream with ¼ cup sugar and set aside.

In a blender, place 1½ cups sugar and the cheese cream and Blend for 5 minutes. Keeping the same blending speed, add the egg yolks, one at a time, at 10-second intervals. Mix for 5 more minutes.

Add the gelatin mixture, increasing the speed to high, and continue blending for 3 minutes more. Pour into a large bowl.

Slowly fold the whipped cream into the cheese mixture with a rubber spatula. Repeat the same step with the beaten egg whites until all the ingredients are thoroughly blended. Set aside.

Make the espresso and sweeten with ½ cup sugar, or to taste. Add the brandy and allow to cool.

In a 12-inch springform pan, layer the cookies uniformly and close together. Moisten with the coffee-brandy mixture. Fill with the cheese mixture and refrigerate overnight.

To serve, shake the cocoa powder generously to cover the top of the Tiramisù. Separate the cake from the pan with a paring knife before opening the release spring.

✩

MIKE'S ON THE AVENUE

NOUVEAU CONTINENTAL FARE
628 St. Charles Avenue
(on the ground floor of the Lafayette Hotel)
New Orleans, Louisiana 70130
(504) 523-1709
Lunch Monday– Friday 11:30 a.m. –2 p.m.
Dinner Daily 6 p.m.–10 p.m.
AVERAGE DINNER FOR TWO: $90

Chef Mike Fennelly borrows flavors from entirely different cuisines and sprinkles them liberally in his Creole concoctions at Mike's on the Avenue. His wildly inventive dishes show traces of regional American, especially that of the Southwest, several Oriental countries and now the contemporary New Orleans mainstream. How do these seemingly clashing styles converge on a dinner plate? In Crawfish Spring Rolls, Filet Mignon with Garlic and Ancho Chile or Grilled Black Beer and Soy Marinated Filet to name a few.

Chef Fennelly's multifaceted artistic contributions extend from his brightly colored, splashy-patterned artwork that decorates the airy restaurant walls to his vibrant edible art—always arranged in a way that manages to be beautiful without being fussy.

Located on St. Charles Avenue with panoramic views of Lafayette Square's majestic oaks, Mike's offers an international selection of fine wines and convenient valet parking.

MIKE'S ON THE AVENUE MENU FOR SIX

Pear Salad

Pomegranate and Rosemary Grilled Lamb Chops

Vanilla Crème Brûlé

Pear Salad

Serves 6
Preparation Time:
15 Minutes

1 Tbsp. sugar
2 Tbsps. Dijon mustard
½ cup balsamic vinegar
1½ tsps. garlic, finely
    chopped
1 tsp. red pepper flakes
1 tsp. salt
2½ cups olive oil
1 lb. baby lettuce mix
18 endive leaves
1 red pear, sliced
½ cup pecans
¼ cup blue cheese,
    crumbled

I n a mixing bowl, combine the sugar, mustard, vinegar, garlic, red pepper flakes and salt. Whisk in the olive oil and adjust the seasonings to taste.

In a salad bowl, toss the greens and vinaigrette together.

Place salad on individual serving plates (in each salad, there should be at least three endive leaves, cut in half lengthwise), and garnish with sliced pears, pecans and blue cheese.

☆

Pomegranate and Rosemary Grilled Lamb Chops

Prepare the marinade by combining the oregano, garlic, rosemary, oil, salt, pepper and pomegranate juice in a mixing bowl. Pour the marinade over the lamb racks and marinate for 24 hours.

Oil and preheat grill for 15 minutes.

Remove the lamb from the marinade and cut into individual chops. Season with salt and pepper and grill 2 to 3 minutes on each side for medium-rare to medium.

Lamb Jelly

In a saucepan, bring the lime juice and sugar to a boil. Remove from heat and add the mint and chile pepper.

Cool and serve with the lamb.

Cooking Secret: Chef Mike Fennelly recommends a wine pairing of Merlot–Stonestreet "Alexander Valley."

Serves 6
Preparation Time:
  20 Minutes
(note marinating time)

- ½ Tbsp. oregano, dry
- ½ cup garlic, chopped
- 2 Tbsps. rosemary, freshly chopped
- 2 cups extra virgin olive oil
- 1 Tbsp. kosher salt
- 1 Tbsp. black pepper
- 2 cups pomegranate juice
- 3 racks of lamb (enough for 6 servings)
  Lamb Jelly (recipe follows)

Lamb Jelly:
- Juice of 7 to 8 limes
- 2½ cups granulated sugar
- ½ tsp. mint, chopped
- 1 serrano chile, seeded and minced (very hot chile)

☆

Vanilla Crème Brûlé

Serves 6
Preparation Time:
  1 Hour
Special Equipment:
  6 custard cups
Preheat oven to 325°

  1 cup sugar
  1 qt. heavy cream
  1 small vanilla bean,
    split
  9 large egg yolks

n a saucepan over low heat combine the sugar, cream and vanilla bean, stirring until the sugar is dissolved. Remove from heat and remove the vanilla bean.

Lightly beat the egg yolks. Slowly add the warm cream to the egg yolks.

Pour into six 8 oz. custard cups and place them in a water bath. (Water should be only halfway up cups).

Cover the pan with foil and bake at 325° for about 35 to 40 minutes.

Check the doneness by shaking the cups, which should not be loose in the center.

★

MR. B's BISTRO

CONTEMPORARY CREOLE
201 Royal Street.
New Orleans, Louisiana 70130
(504) 523-2078
Dinner Daily 5:30 p.m.–10 p.m.
Lunch Daily 11:30 a.m.–3 p.m.
AVERAGE DINNER FOR TWO: $55

Since 1979, Mr. B's has been redefining New Orleans cooking to revive the distinct qualities of Louisiana's varied cultural influences by using local and regional ingredients. The result is innovative, simple, straightforward culinary creations. Quality and farm freshness predominate with homemade sausages, cured and smoked meats and chutneys served up bistro style.

The menu includes a generous selection of classic Creole dishes such as Pasta Jambalaya, consisting of Gulf Shrimp, Andouille, Oven-Roasted Duck and Chicken, tossed with Spinach Fettuccine. A local seafood appetizer is the Louisiana Seafood Tower, featuring a trio of favorites that includes Marinated Blue Crab Claws, Fried Oysters and Crab Cakes. The Creole Catfish is rolled in cornmeal and sautéed, served with Black-Eyed Peas seasoned with a Sausage and Tomato Tartar Sauce. Desserts are highlighted by Mr. B's famous Chocolate Caramel Pecan Cake brimming with layers of Caramel, Chocolate Mousse and Louisiana Pecans. The Bread Pudding is a Brennan family recipe rich in eggs, cream and butter, served warm with an Irish Whiskey Sauce.

RECIPE SECRETS FROM MR. B'S BISTRO

Gumbo Ya Ya

Gumbo Ya Ya

Serves 4
Preparation Time:
 45 Minutes

½ cup oil
3 Tbsps. flour
1 lb. andouille sausage,
   chopped into 1-inch
   chunks
1 medium onion,
   chopped
1 medium green pepper,
   chopped
1 Tbsp. butter
2 cups chicken stock
1 cup diced chicken
   Salt and pepper to
   taste
2 tsps. filé powder
½ cup water
4 cups rice, cooked

To make the roux, heat the oil in a saucepan. Add the flour and cook until it turns a dark brown. Set aside.

In another saucepan, sauté the andouille sausage, onion and green pepper in butter for approximately 10 minutes.

Add the chicken stock and simmer for 10 minutes. Bring the mixture to a rolling boil. Add the roux and let simmer for 20 minutes.

Add the chicken and season to taste.

Dissolve the filé powder in the half cup water and add to the soup. Simmer for 10 minutes and serve over hot rice.

☆

PALACE CAFÉ

CONTEMPORARY CREOLE SEAFOOD
605 Canal Street
New Orleans, Louisiana
(504) 523-1661
Dinner Daily 5:30 p.m.–10 p.m.
Lunch Daily 11:30 a.m.–2:30 p.m.
Sunday Brunch 10:30 a.m.–2:30 p.m.
AVERAGE DINNER FOR TWO: $75

The Palace Café is the New Orleans version of one of the grand cafés of Paris. The food is real basic food that stays within the boundaries of New Orleans tradition. Chef Robert Bruce focuses his menu to highlight local ingredients, which means you won't find any foie gras and truffles. The food is clean, straightforward, less fussy and definitely a lot cheaper.

Some of the must-tries on the menu are a Pan-Roasted Oyster appetizer, poached in a light Rosemary-Infused Cream, then topped with Romano Cheese and Bread Crumbs. Bruce's Gumbo is brimming with flavors enhanced with Gulf Seafood, Okra, Peppers and Garlic. The Soft-Shell Crabs are flash-fried until crisp, then served with a fragrant Ragout made from fresh Corn and Mirlitons and finished off with a Spicy Hot Tasso Ham and drizzled with a Hollandaise spiked with Red Onions.

One section of the menu is devoted to tempting entrée salads offering a choice of Jumbo Shrimp in Rémoulade Dressing with Roasted Tomatoes on a bed of Baby Greens, or a Roasted Chicken tossed with a Citrus Essence, Creole Mustard, Spinach, Pepper and Roasted Pecans or Bruce's signature Crabmeat Cheesecake in a pool of Creole Sauce Meunière atop baby lettuce with a light drizzle of Balsamic-Lime Vinaigrette.

Save room for desserts, with tempting selections such as the Louisiana Root Beer Float with housemade sugar-cane ice cream and Bananas Foster Shortcake, Bourbon Pecan Pie and the famous White Chocolate Bread Pudding, created with white chocolate baked inside the bread pudding and smothered with a warm white chocolate sauce.

RECIPE SECRETS FROM PALACE CAFÉ

Oyster Six Shot

Mango, Strawberry and Opal Basil Sorbet

Oyster Six Shot

Serves 4
Preparation Time:
  45 Minutes

Peppercorn Mignonette:
Yield: 1½ cups
  2 shallots, peeled,
    minced
  ½ cup red wine vinegar
  5 Tbsps. Creole mustard
  1 Tbsp. cracked black
    pepper
  1 tsp. salt
1½ cups salad oil

Cajun-Mary Sauce:
Yield: 1½ cups
  1 cup tomato juice
  ½ cup tomato paste
  1 tsp. Tabasco Sauce
  3 Tbsps. Worcestershire
    sauce
  ¼ cup lemon juice
  ½ tsp. ground celery
    seeds
    Salt and ground black
    pepper to taste
    Creole seasoning to
    taste

24 raw oysters
  4 lemon crowns, garnish
  1 Tbsp. parsley, chopped,
    garnish
24 chilled shot glasses

or the Peppercorn Mignonette: Combine all the ingredients except the oil in a blender. With the blender still running, slowly add the oil to emulsify. Set aside.

For the Cajun-Mary Sauce: In a mixing bowl combine all the ingredients. Season to taste with salt, pepper and Creole seasoning.

To assemble, place 1 oyster in each of the 24 shot glasses. Top 12 of the oysters with 1 Tbsp. of the Peppercorn Mignotte. Top the other 12 with 1 Tbsp. of the Cajun-Mary Sauce.

Place 6 shot glasses on each of 4 large plates: 3 with Peppercorn Mignonette and 3 with Cajun-Mary Sauce. Garnish with a lemon crown in the center of the plate and a sprinkling of parsley.

Mango, Strawberry and Opal Basil Sorbet

Clean and hull the strawberries. Sprinkle with sugar and toss to coat berries.

Combine the mango purée, lime juice and syrup in a large bowl.

Purée the basil with a small amount of syrup mixture in a blender and strain to remove the basil leaves, then return purée to the rest of the syrup mixture.

Purée the strawberries in a blender and strain, removing all fibers. Add the berries to the syrup mixture and combine.

Process according to ice cream machine instructions. Freeze for 24 hours.

Yield: 2 quarts
Preparation Time:
  30 Minutes
(note freezing time)

  8 **cups strawberries**
 ½ **cup sugar**
  2 **cups mango purée**
  1 **cup fresh lime juice**
  3 **cups simple syrup**
     (equal parts sugar and
     water by volume)
 ¼ **Tbsp. opal basil**

☆

PERISTYLE

AMERICAN BISTRO FARE
1041 Dumaine Street
New Orleans, Louisiana 70116
504 593-9535
Dinner Monday–Saturday 6 p.m.–11 p.m.
Lunch Fridays 11:30 p.m.–2 p.m. (Limited seating)
AVERAGE DINNER FOR TWO: $90

Almost exclusively American Bistro fare, Chef Anne Kearney's menu creations employ influences of Southern France and Northern Italy in both preparation and presentation. Menu changes are seasonal and incorporate the best of the region's fish, game, fowl and shellfish as well as home-grown herbs, fresh produce and seasonal specialties from local suppliers and purveyors. Although Peristyle's cuisine is classically styled Provençal fare of the highest standards, Chef Kearney's patrons will tell you her cuisine is, first and always, "food of love."

Peristyle takes its name from the Peristyle at New Orleans' City Park (any oval structure of columns is known as a peristyle). Located on the ground floor of a 19th-century French Quarter structure, the wrought-iron balcony overlooks New Orleans' Armstrong Park. A grand old mahogany bar frames a stunning portrait of the Peristyle itself. The bar's polished copper top, fresh flowers and a row of hopper-transom windows above the bar's banquette make for a decidedly romantic welcome—day or night.

RECIPE SECRETS FROM PERISTYLE

Gratin of Gulf Oysters and Baby Artichokes in Brandy-Dijon Cream

Jumbo Lump Crab Meat with Horseradish Dressing, Chilled Roasted Beets and Pickled Red Onions

Gratin of Gulf Oysters and Baby Artichokes in a Brandy-Dijon Cream

To prepare the Brandy-Dijon Cream Sauce, melt the butter, add the flour and cook for 1 minute. Add the white wine and cook for 1 minute more. Add the Dijon, brandy, cream and milk, stirring constantly. Reduce to a simmer and cook for 20 minutes. Season, strain and chill until needed.

Mix bread crumbs, Parmesan cheese, parsley, lemon zest, olive oil and seasonings. Set aside.

Cover the bottom of a large casserole dish with half the sauce. Arrange the artichoke hearts, points touching the center, atop the sauce. Place the oysters on top of the artichokes and top with the remaining sauce. Sprinkle generously with the bread crumb mixture and bake at 400° for 15 minutes or until brown and heated through. Garnish with chopped parsley.

Serves 4
Preparation Time:
  45 Minutes
Preheat oven to 400°

  2 Tbsps. butter
  2 Tbsps. flour
  ¼ cup white wine
  1½ Tbsps. Dijon mustard
  1½ Tbsps. brandy
  ¾ cup cream
  ¼ cup milk
    Salt and white pepper
  ¼ cup coarse bread
    crumbs
  2 Tbsps. Parmesan
    cheese, hand grated
  1½ tsps. parsley, chopped
  1½ tsps. lemon zest,
    chopped
    Olive oil to moisten
    Salt and white pepper
  16 artichoke hearts
  20 oysters

☆

Jumbo Lump Crab Meat with Horseradish Dressing, Chilled Roasted Beets and Pickled Red Onions

Serves 4
Preparation Time:
 1 Hour
Preheat oven to 350°

- ½ lb. beets, small and uniformly sized
- 2 Tbsps. rice vinegar
  Salt and white pepper
- 2 Tbsps. olive oil
- 1 large red onion, cored and halved
- 1 Tbsp. kosher salt
- ½ cup water
- ½ cup rice vinegar
- 1½ tsps. kosher salt
- 2 thick strips of orange zest
- 5 coriander seeds, crushed
- 3 white peppercorns
- ⅛ tsp. mustard seed
- ½ lb. jumbo lump crab meat
- 4 Tbsps. Sour Cream-Mayonnaise (recipe follows on next page)
  Generous pinch of finely chopped chives
  Fresh prepared horseradish to taste
- 4 Tbsps. herb salad mix (recipe follows on next page)

Remove the very end of each beet and place them, cut side down, in a shallow baking pan. Fill the pan with about ½ inch water. Cover with foil and roast until tender—about 30 minutes at 350°. Remove from the water and cool slightly. Reserve ¼ cup of the pretty beet water. Carefully remove the skins. Slice the beets ¼-inch thick (thinner if possible). Place in a small bowl and gently move around in a marinade made with the reserved beet water, 2 Tbsps. rice vinegar, seasonings and oil. Allow to marinate for 30 minutes. Strain juice and store in squirt bottle for presentation purposes. Chill beets until needed.

Thinly slice julienne strips from red onion. Toss the onion strips with kosher salt and set aside.

Prepare the brine in a small saucepan by bringing the water, rice vinegar, kosher salt, orange zest, coriander, peppercorns and mustard seed to a boil.

Remove from heat and cool for 10 minutes. Rinse the onions in cold water and drain. While the brine is still warm, strain the liquid over the sliced onions and stir to coat. Cool and store.

Mix crab, Sour Cream-Mayonnaise Blend, chopped chives, salt, white pepper and as much horseradish as you dare together in a small stainless steel bowl.

To serve, arrange the beets on the base of each individual plate, slightly overlapping in a circle. Top with a little mound of onions. Place a tall mound of crab salad, topped with the herb salad mix.

☆

Sour Cream-Mayonnaise

Make the mayonnaise: Put the egg, lemon juice, salt and pepper in a food processor and process for 15 seconds. With the motor running, slowly pour in the oil through the feed tube and process until the mayonnaise has thickened. Transfer to a bowl. Add sour cream and blend well.

Cover and refrigerate, if you are making the mayonnaise ahead.

Herb Salad
Mix all ingredients together.

1 egg
1 Tbsp. lemon juice
  Salt and white pepper
1 cup olive oil
1½ cups sour cream

Herb Salad:
  1 tsp. fresh chives, cut in
    ½-inch snips
  2 tsps. parsley leaves,
    flat, chopped
  1 tsp. fresh tarragon
  1 tsp. olive oil
  1 tsp. salt

RED FISH GRILL

CREOLE
115 Bourbon Street
New Orleans, Louisiana 70130
(504) 598-1200
http://www.redfishgrill.com
Lunch Monday–Saturday 11 a.m.–3 p.m.
Dinner Daily 5 p.m.–11 p.m.
AVERAGE DINNER FOR TWO: $60.00

L ocated at the gateway to Bourbon Street, the Red Fish Grill, under the culinary direction of Executive Chef Mitch Engleman, boasts a variety of fresh seafood selections. Choices include an abundant supply of fresh Gulf shellfish, an oyster bar and several other New Orleans classic seafood dishes like Baked Oysters, Crawfish Étouffée, and Barbecue Shrimp Po' Boys.

The menu layout whimsically arranges food items in several original categories such as *bait* (appetizers, soups and salads), *Fin Fish, Shell Fish, Go Fish* (meat, pasta, vegetarian) and *Overboard* (dessert).

In the center of the state-of-the-art kitchen is a hickory-wood-burning grill, which imparts a smoky flavor and taste to seafoods, meats and their fresh vegetables.

The dining area is graced with sculpted palms extending from tall columns. Shellfish of all shapes and sizes are etched into a sea-colored concrete floor and hand-painted tables provide colorful drama for the eye. A lively jazz brunch is served on Sundays.

RECIPE SECRETS FROM THE RED FISH GRILL

Sweet Potato Catfish with Andouille Cream Drizzle

Grilled Vegetable Po' Boy

Peanut Butter Pie

Sweet Potato Catfish with Andouille Cream Drizzle

Sprinkle the catfish with 1 tsp. salt and 1 tsp. Creole seasoning. Set aside.

Peel and place roasted sweet potato flesh along with 1 tsp. salt, ½ tsp. Creole seasoning, mayonnaise, pepper and bread crumbs in a mixer and blend. Spread the sweet potato crust on top of the fish.

In a hot, ovenproof skillet, put ¼ cup of the clarified butter and sauté the fish, crust side up.

Place the skillet under the broiler and cook until the fish is nicely browned.

Sauté spinach in ¼ cup clarified butter and season with ½ tsp. Creole seasoning, salt and pepper to taste. Drain the spinach and place in the center of each plate.

Place the catfish on top, allowing the spinach to be seen on either side of the fish. Drizzle the sauce around the fish and spinach.

Andouille Cream Drizzle

Sauté the sausage in oil until lightly browned. Add the Creole seasoning. Deglaze with bourbon and reduce the sauce by half. Add the honey and the cream. Add the roux and let simmer until the flour taste is gone. Salt and pepper to taste.

Serves 4
Preparation Time:
  30 Minutes

4 catfish fillet, 8 to 9 oz. each, trimmed
2 tsps. salt
2 tsps. Creole seasoning (recommend Paul Prudhomme's)
5 lbs. roasted sweet potato flesh
2 cups mayonnaise
Black pepper to taste
½ cup bread crumbs
½ cup (1 stick) butter, clarified
¾ lb. spinach, cleaned
¾ cup Andouille Cream Drizzle (recipe follows)
Green onions, chopped, for garnish

Andouille Cream Drizzle:
½ lb. andouille sausage, diced into ¼-inch pieces
3 Tbsps. vegetable oil
2 Tbsps. Creole seasoning
⅓ cup bourbon
2 Tbsps. honey
1 qt. heavy cream
3 Tbsps. blond roux

☆

Grilled Vegetable Po' Boy

Yield: 2 sandwiches
Preparation Time:
30 Minutes

1 cup olive oil
⅓ cup rice vinegar
¼ tsp. salt
   Dash black pepper
½ tsp. fresh rosemary,
   chopped
1½ Tbsps. fresh garlic,
   chopped

4 Japanese eggplants,
   halved and peeled
1 red onion, sliced
   ½-inch thick
1 zucchini, sliced ¼-inch
   thick
½ roasted red pepper
3 oz. fontina cheese
2 cups roasted garlic
   cloves
⅔ cup mayonnaise
1½ tsps. salt
½ tsp. black pepper
2 po' boy loaves (small
   loaves of Italian or
   French bread)
¼ cup lettuce, julienned
1 tomato, sliced

I n a large mixing bowl, combine the olive oil, vinegar, salt, pepper, rosemary and garlic. Add the vegetables to the marinade. Drain well, reserving the marinade, and grill the eggplant, red onion and zucchini until tender. Do not char.

Place the eggplants, grilled onion, zucchini and roasted bell pepper in an ovenproof skillet. Heat. Top with fontina cheese and melt under broiler.

In a blender or food processor combine the roasted garlic cloves, mayonnaise, salt and pepper.

Slice the po' boy loaves lengthwise and spread with the roasted garlic mixture. Top with the hot vegetables, lettuce and tomato. Slice in half on the bias and serve.

☆

Peanut Butter Pie

ombine all ingredients and press evenly into a 10-inch pie pan, making all edges even. Bake 8 minutes in a 350° oven. Cool completely.

Peanut Butter Filling

In a mixing bowl, whip together the butter, sugar, peanut butter, cream cheese and vanilla. Beat in the egg.

Place a layer of the peanut butter filling in the crust, using half the filling. Drizzle the Ganache on top of the filling. Freeze.

Add the remaining layer of peanut butter filling. Garnish with chopped peanuts. Chill.

Ganache

In a saucepan over medium heat, combine the cream and corn syrup. Remove from heat and add the chocolate. Stir in the butter.

Yield: 1 Pie
Preparation Time:
   30 Minutes
(note refrigeration time)
Preheat oven to 350°

Pie Crust:
   1 cup crushed pretzels
   ¼ cup semisweet
      chocolate, finely
      chopped
   ¼ cup sugar
   ½ cup melted butter

Peanut Butter Filling:
   1 lb. butter
   1¼ lbs. confectioners'
      sugar
   1 lb. peanut butter
   ½ lb. cream cheese
   ¼ tsp. vanilla
   1 egg
      Ganache (recipe
      follows)
   ½ cup peanuts, chopped

Ganache:
Yield: 3½ cups
   1 cup heavy cream
   ¼ cup corn syrup
   1 lb. semisweet
      chocolate
   4 Tbsps. butter

★

UPPERLINE

CREOLE CUISINE
1413 Upperline Street
New Orleans, Louisiana 70115
(504) 891-9822
Dinner Wednesday–Sunday 5:30 p.m.–9:30 p.m.
Brunch Sunday 11:30 a.m.–2 p.m.
AVERAGE DINNER FOR TWO: $75

This trend-setting Uptown bistro is an oasis of Creole hospitality and one of the friendliest fine dining spots in town. Set in a beautiful 1877 townhouse with whitewashed walls, art deco lighting fixtures, local folk art and fresh flowers, Upperline is a New Orleans feast for all the senses.

Executive Chef Richard Benz creates adventurous cuisine, blending traditional Creole flavors that are stylishly infused with contemporary, trend-setting freshness. Most popular with the locals are the roast duck and the great variety of seafood. House specialties include the *original* Fried Green Tomatoes with Shrimp Rémoulade, Spicy Shrimp with Jalapeño Corn Bread and Duck Étouffée.

Casual dining matches friendly, competent service with a hallmark wine list. Distinctive and coveted wines from throughout the world are offered at modest prices, earning Upperline the Wine Spectator Award of Excellence for two consecutive years.

Upperline has inspired *Southern Living* magazine to say, "If you can eat at only one fine restaurant in New Orleans, make it the Upperline."

RECIPE SECRETS FROM UPPERLINE

Fried Green Tomatoes with Shrimp Rémoulade

Roasted Garlic Soup

Roast Duck with Ginger Peach Sauce

Honey-Pecan Bread Pudding with Caramel Sauce

Fried Green Tomatoes with Shrimp Rémoulade

Peel shrimp and set aside. Simmer shells, wine, onion, bay leaf, celery, cayenne and peppercorns in 2 cups water for 30 minutes, then strain through a fine strainer. Bring stock to a boil, add the peeled shrimp, bring to a boil again and cook for 1 to 2 minutes. Check one shrimp to see if it is cooked and translucence is gone. Do not overcook. Strain saving stock for soup. Plunge shrimp into iced water, drain, cover and refrigerate until serving time.

Slice green tomatoes ½- to ¾-inch thick.

Prepare the egg wash by mixing together egg and milk.

Season cornmeal with salt and pepper. Dip the tomato slices in the egg wash and then coat with cornmeal.

Heat a small amount of oil in a heavy sauté pan and cook slowly until golden brown, then turn and brown the other side. If cooked too fast the outside gets too brown before the inside is cooked.

Place 2 slices tomato next to each other on individual serving plate. Top each slice with 3 or 4 chilled, cooked shrimp, and top each slice with approximately 1½ to 2 Tbsps. rémoulade sauce.

Serves 8
Preparation Time:
  45 Minutes

  3 lbs. medium shrimp
    (in the shell)
    Shrimp shells
 ½ cup white wine
  1 small white onion,
    peeled
  1 bay leaf
  1 stalk celery
 ½ tsp. cayenne
  6 peppercorns
  2 cups water
  4 green tomatoes
  1 egg
  1 cup milk
  1 cup cornmeal
    Salt and pepper to
    taste
  4 Tbsps. light olive oil
  2 cups New Orleans Red
    Rémoulade (recipe
    follows on next page)

☆

New Orleans Red Rémoulade

Yield: 4 cups
Preparation Time:
  15 Minutes

  1 cup light salad oil
  1 cup virgin olive oil
  ¾ cup Creole mustard
  ¾ Tbsp. garlic, finely
      chopped
  4 tsps. paprika
  2 Tbsps. Tabasco Sauce
      or to taste
  ⅛ cup parsley, chopped
1½ Tbsps. sugar
  ½ cup green onion tops,
      finely chopped
1½ Tbsps. Worcestershire
      sauce
1½ Tbsps. lemon juice
  ¼ cup ketchup
  ⅓ cup horseradish
  1 Tbsp. white onion,
      grated
1½ tsps. garlic powder
  ½ cup celery, finely
      chopped

 Mix all ingredients together in a large mixing bowl. Taste and adjust the seasoning.
    Keep refrigerated until use.

Cooking Secret: Rémoulade sauce should be tangy and have a perky taste. More Tabasco Sauce can be used to obtain the desired flavor. Covered and chilled, it will keep about 3 weeks.

☆

Roasted Garlic Soup

I n a heavy-gauge sauce pot, heat the oil and brown the garlic over medium heat.

Add the onions and cook until they are softened, about 5 minutes. Add the stock and potatoes and simmer for 30 minutes. Season to taste with salt and pepper. Add the cream. Purée and serve.

Serves 6
Preparation Time:
  45 Minutes

2 Tbsps. olive oil
2 cups garlic cloves, peeled
2 onions, sliced
1 qt. chicken stock
2 baking potatoes, peeled and sliced
  Salt and pepper to taste
1 cup cream

Roast Duck with Ginger Peach Sauce

Serves 4
Preparation Time:
1½ Hours
Preheat oven to 400°

2 medium ducks, 4 to
   5 lbs. each
4 Tbsps. soy sauce
4 Tbsps. Dijon mustard
   Kosher salt
1 Tbsp. dry thyme
1 Tbsp. puréed garlic
1 Tbsp. cracked black
   pepper
1 lb. summer peaches
½ cup water
2 Tbsps. fresh ginger,
   minced
½ cup mango chutney
1 cup orange juice

Remove excess skin, giblets and wingtips from ducks. Place ducks on a rack in a roasting pan. Pierce the skin with a fork all over. Rub soy sauce over the skin, then rub on the mustard. Coat well with salt, thyme, garlic and pepper.

Bake for 45 minutes at 400°, then turn the ducks over. Reduce heat to 350° and roast for 30 minutes longer. Remove ducks from oven and let cool enough to handle. Split ducks in half and remove the rib bones.

Peel and cube peaches and cook in a saucepan with water, ginger, chutney and orange juice over medium heat. Bring to a simmer and reduce by half.

Serve the ginger peach sauce over warm duck.

☆

Honey-Pecan Bread Pudding with Caramel Sauce

Tear the bread into small pieces. Set aside.

In a mixing bowl, mix together the eggs, milk, 1 cup sugar, honey, vanilla and cinnamon.

Place bread in a shallow baking dish. Pour the egg mixture over the bread and gently mix until the bread is uniformly wet. Scatter pecans over top evenly and press gently into the mixture. Bake at 350° for 1 hour or until the pudding is semi-firm.

Prepare the caramel sauce in a heavy-gauge sauce pan, over medium heat. Heat 1 cup sugar until melted. Continue cooking until it is a rich dark caramel color. Remove from stove and stir to cool for 5 minutes.

Add the cream and cook until it coats a spoon.

Serve over warm bread pudding.

Serves 6
Preparation Time:
  1 Hour 15 Minutes
Preheat oven to 350°

  1 loaf day-old French
    bread (baguette)
  4 eggs
  1 pt. milk
  2 cups sugar
  $\frac{1}{2}$ cup honey
  1 tsp. vanilla
  1 tsp. cinnamon
  1 cup pecan halves
  $\frac{1}{3}$ cup heavy cream

CHATEAU SONESTA HOTEL

800 Iberville Street
New Orleans, Louisiana 70112
(800) SONESTA
(504) 586-0800
ROOM RATES: $140–$750 (for the two-bedroom suite)

C hateau Sonesta Hotel is located at the site of the former D. H. Holmes Canal Street Department Store which was constructed in 1849. The transformation of this pre-Civil War landmark building into a 20th century hotel includes a complete interior renovation and exterior restoration to the building's 1913 facade. The look is late Italianate in character, with bay windows separated by ornately detailed cast-iron mullion that extends to the underside of the cornices.

Generations of New Orleanians used to meet friends and family under the D.H. Holmes clock. Today, guests of Chateau Sonesta carry on the time-honored tradition by meeting at The Clock Bar—appropriately named for the timepiece that now occupies a place of honor in the popular lounge.

The 250 spacious rooms and suites feature 12-foot ceilings, queen or king beds and views overlooking Bourbon Street, Dauphine Street or the interior pool and courtyard areas. More than 300 original works of art decorate the Chateau, assuring every room has lagniappe or something special.

Menu highlights feature French, Creole and American cuisine in an atmosphere of historic style and contemporary comfort.

Corn and Crab Meat Chowder

In a large saucepan over medium heat, sauté the celery, green and red peppers, onion, shallot, garlic and chopped clams in the butter until tender. Add the flour and stir.

Add the white wine, clam juice, Worcestershire, water and ½ cup sherry. Keep stirring and heat sauce to boiling. Reduce heat to low. Add the jerk seasoning and simmer for 20 to 30 minutes, stirring occasionally.

Add the corn and heavy cream and cook for another 8 to 10 minutes on low heat, continuing to stir. Check the consistency. The chowder should be very creamy. If sufficiently creamy, add remaining sherry. If it is too liquid, use some arrow root diluted with the last ½ cup of sherry and cook over low heat for a few more minutes until thick and creamy.

Add the crab meat and serve.

Serves 12
Preparation Time:
  45 Minutes

- 3 cups celery, finely chopped
- 2 cups green bell pepper, finely chopped
- 2 cups red bell pepper, diced
- 2 cups onion, finely chopped
- 1 cup shallot, finely chopped
- 2 Tbsps. garlic, finely chopped
- 1 cup chopped clams (optional)
- 16 Tbsps. (2 sticks) butter
- 1 cup flour
- 1 qt. white wine
- 1 qt. clam juice
- 2 Tbsps. Worcestershire sauce
- 1 qt. water
- 1 cup sherry
- ½ cup jerk seasoning or to taste
- 2 lbs. cut corn, frozen
- 1 qt. heavy cream
- Salt to taste (be careful—clam juice contains sodium)
- Arrowroot for finishing
- 1 lb. lump crab meat, picked over

☆

ELLIOTT HOUSE BED AND BREAKFAST

801 North Duncan Avenue
Amite, Louisiana 70422
(504) 748-8553
ROOM RATES: $60–$110

One of Amite's earliest homes, nestled deep among oaks, pines and camellias on a spacious four-acre lot, the Elliott House greets you as you circle through the wooded driveway. The long gallery is classically framed by fifteen solid cypress columns.

In the spirit of the Elliott House's turn-of-the-century graciousness (it was built in the 1880's), you will find beautifully restored original cypress shutters, heart pine floors and family heirlooms throughout.

Although the Elliott House has central heat and air, two of the five guest rooms have working fireplaces for cozy, romantic evenings, and each high-ceilinged room has a fan for those sultry Louisiana summers. Awake to freshly brewed Louisiana coffee and a full breakfast featuring the favorite family recipes of hosts Joe and Flora Landwehr's.

Elliott House is conveniently located near area attractions, excursions and activities, or guests may choose to spend time rocking or swinging right outside the front door.

Apricot-Prune Coffee Cake

Butter and flour a tube pan.

Coarsely chop the apricots and prunes. Sift 3 cups flour, baking powder, baking soda and salt into a large mixing bowl. In a separate bowl, beat the ¾ cup of butter until fluffy. Stir in the sugar and eggs. Add the vanilla and blend into the flour mixture Stir in the sour cream. Gently fold in the prunes and apricots, then the nuts.

In a separate bowl, mix together the light brown sugar, 2 Tbsps. butter, 2 Tbsps. flour and cinnamon to make a streusel. Set aside.

Turn ⅓ of the batter into the prepared tube pan. Sprinkle with ⅓ of the streusel mixture. Repeat layering twice, ending with a topping of streusel.

Bake 55 to 60 minutes at 350°. Let cool in pan 20 minutes and remove from pan. Sift powdered sugar on top before serving.

Serves 10
Preparation Time:
  1½ Hours
Preheat oven to 350°

  ¾ cup dried apricots
  ¾ cup dried prunes,
    pitted
  3 cups + 2 Tbsps.
    unsifted all-purpose
    flour
  ½ Tbsp. baking powder
  ¾ tsp. baking soda
  ¼ tsp. salt
  ¾ cup + 2 Tbsps. softened
    butter
1½ cups sugar
  4 eggs, beaten
  ½ Tbsp. vanilla
  1 cup sour cream
  ¾ cup pecans, chopped
  ½ cup light brown sugar
  1 tsp. cinnamon
  2 Tbsps. powdered sugar

☆

Granola

Yield: 8 Cups
Preparation Time:
30 Minutes
Preheat oven to 350°

1 heaping Tbsp. peanut
  butter
²⁄₃ cup honey
½ cup canola oil
3 cups old fashioned
  rolled oats
1 cup wheat germ
¾ cup sunflower seed
  kernels
½ cup sliced almonds

I n a mixing bowl combine the peanut butter, honey and oil, mixing thoroughly. Add the oats, wheat germ, sunflower seeds and almonds.

Bake in a 350° oven on an oiled cookie sheet for 20 minutes, turning the granola over after about 10 minutes. It should be toasted and golden.

Delicious as a cereal or as a topping over yogurt and fruit.

Dutch Baby

Beat eggs in a mixing bowl at medium speed. Gradually add the flour and salt, blending well. Add the milk and blend thoroughly.

Spread the bottom and sides of a cast-iron skillet with 3 Tbsps. melted butter. Pour in the batter and bake in a pre-heated 450° oven until the crust is brown, about 20 minutes.

Mix the lemon juice with the remaining 3 Tbsps. butter and add the syrup.

Pour the syrup over the Dutch Baby and sprinkle with con-fectioners' sugar. Jelly or preserves may be used in place of syrup.

Cooking Secret: This dish is a cross between an omelet and a soufflé. It puffs during the cooling, but falls when served.

Serves 4
Preparation Time:
 30 Minutes
Preheat oven to 450°

  3 **eggs**
 $\frac{1}{2}$ **cup sifted flour**
 $\frac{1}{2}$ **tsp. salt**
 $\frac{1}{2}$ **cup milk**
  6 **Tbsps. melted butter**
 $\frac{1}{2}$ **lemon**
 $\frac{1}{4}$ **cup cane syrup**
    Confectioners' sugar

☆

FAIRCHILD HOUSE

1518 Prytania Street
New Orleans, Louisiana 70130
(800) 256-8096
(504) 524-0152
ROOM RATES: $75–$125

One of New Orleans' architectural treasures, Fairchild House was established in an 1841 Greek Revival home with two adjacent guest houses. Situated among the picturesque oaks of the lower Garden District, this bed and breakfast is in the heart of the Mardi Gras Parade route, offering easy streetcar access to the French Quarter.

Fairchild House offers 14 rooms, each with a private bath, in-room television, telephone with voice mail, and decorated with elegant antiques, evoking the Victorian period.

Complimentary wine and cheese are served upon arrival and a continental breakfast is offered with seasonal fruits, assorted breads, coffee and tea.

Crayfish Arlesienne

Cut the butter squash in half lengthwise, remove the seeds, and cook the squash in boiling water or steam until tender and crisp, about 10 minutes. Set aside.

In a sauté pan, melt the butter. Add the olive oil, onion, green pepper, green onions and garlic. Sauté over medium heat for about 5 to 7 minutes.

Add the tomato purée, white pepper and Worcestershire. Bring to a boil. Let simmer over low heat for 20 minutes.

Add the crawfish and flour. Cook for 3 minutes. Remove from heat and add the coconut milk.

Fill the cavity of each squash with the crawfish mixture and sprinkle with bread crumbs and grated cheese.

Bake for 15 minutes at 350°.

Cooking Secret: Shrimp is a delicious substitute for the crayfish.

Serves 6
Preparation Time:
 45 Minutes
Preheat oven to 350°

- 3 butter squash
- ½ stick butter
- 1 Tbsp. olive oil
- 1 onion, chopped
- 1 green pepper, chopped
- 1 bunch green onions, chopped
- 4 to 6 garlic cloves, mashed
- ¾ cup tomato purée
- ⅛ tsp. white pepper
- 1 Tbsp. Worcestershire sauce
- 1 lb. crawfish tails, cooked
- 2 Tbsps. flour
- 4 Tbsps. unsweetened coconut milk
  Bread crumbs to taste
  Grated mozzarella cheese to taste

☆

HOTEL MAISON DE VILLE

727 Rue Toulouse
New Orleans, Louisiana 70130
(800) 634-1600
(504) 561-5858
ROOM RATES: $165–$825

I n the heart of the French Quarter, Maison de Ville is one of the most romantic destinations in the country. High ceilings, antiques, four-poster beds and period paintings are just some of the touches that give the main house a luxurious feeling. Accommodations reflect a different phase of the genteel Southern lifestyle: some are refined, some are rustic. The antiques are individualized and fit each setting.

Built circa 1788 by American naturalist John James Audubon for his family, the Audubon Cottages are where he created many of his wildlife masterpieces. All the historic cottages, situated around a swimming pool, have private courtyards, rare antiques and Audubon prints.

The Bistro at Maison de Ville is small, but the experience is luscious, flavorful and diverse. The white-clothed tables stand beside bentwood café chairs in the middle of the dark hardwood floor. Fans spin overhead and light jazz fills the air as diners enjoy the cuisine.

Chef Greg Picolo creates a menu filled with mouth-watering dishes. Among the highlights are Escargots Bourguignon, Roasted Eggplant and Coconut Soup, Sea Scallops with Wild Mushroom Galette, Chocolate Crème Brulée and Lemon-Basil Sorbet.

Oysters, Spinach and Goat Cheese Beggars Purse with Apple-Smoked Bacon Vinaigrette

Drain oysters in a colander and reserve the juice. Sauté the oysters in 2 Tbsps. of butter with half of the onion and half of the garlic. Cook briefly until edges of oysters curl, then let cool.

Sauté the spinach in 4 Tbsps. of butter, with the remaining onions and garlic until barely wilted. Add the oyster juice, Pernod, nutmeg, salt and pepper and sauté until the spinach is cooked and has absorbed the liquid. Place in a colander to allow excess moisture to drain. Set aside and let the mixture cool.

Melt the remaining butter. Prepare the Phyllo by layering 4 sheets, each brushed with butter.

Place 2 Tbsps. of cooled spinach, four oysters and 1 Tbsp. of goat cheese in the center of the Phyllo. Bring ends of pastry up onto its center, like a purse, using additional butter to seal the pastry. Bake for 12 minutes at 375° until brown.

Cook bacon well, until very crispy. Remove bacon bits from pan and reserve on paper towel. Combine warm bacon oil with mustard, lemon juice, salt and black pepper in a mixer and blend to create an emulsion.

Place the hot beggar purse on a bed of mixed greens, drizzle with vinaigrette and garnish with the bacon bits.

Serves 8
Preparation Time:
 1 Hour
Preheat oven to 375°

32 oysters
1 lb. butter
1 lb. onion, minced fine
3 Tbsps. fresh garlic, chopped
2 lbs. fresh spinach, washed, stems removed
1 Tbsp. Pernod
1 tsp. nutmeg
 Salt and pepper to taste
32 Phyllo sheets
1 lb. goat cheese
¾ lb. apple-smoked bacon, diced
2 Tbsps. Creole or whole grain mustard
 Juice from 1 lemon

☆

Crawfish and Mushroom Gumbo

Serves 4
Preparation Time:
 2 Hours

1½ cup light blond roux
   (½ cup of butter and
   1 cup of flour)
5 onions, finely chopped
3 celery stalks, finely
   chopped
1 green bell pepper,
   finely chopped
2 red bell peppers, finely
   chopped
6 tsps. garlic, minced
   fine
4 cups chicken stock
2 cups reduced shrimp
   or crawfish stock
1 cup veal demi-glaze
3 lbs. crawfish tails
2 cups Madeira wine
3 lbs. shiitake
   mushrooms, chopped
   Salt and pepper to
   taste

Prepare a roux by combining the butter and flour in a heavy saucepan. Cook over moderate heat until mixture turns light caramel color. Be sure to stir mixture constantly, as it can burn easily.

Add all the chopped vegetables to the roux. Sauté until tender. Add the garlic. With a wire whisk, slowly add the chicken and shrimp stocks, demi-glaze and wine to the roux and vegetable mixture until all stock is incorporated.

Cook for 45 minutes in saucepan, Sauté crawfish tails with mushrooms in a small amount of butter and oil. Add to stock mixture and let simmer for an additional 30 seconds.

Cooking Secret: Serve the Gumbo over rice, preferably pecan or wild rice.

Grilled Shrimps in a Creole Tomato Sauce with Andouille, Shiitake and Acorn Squash Orzo

Sauté ⅔ of the onions, bell pepper, celery and bay leaves until onions are clear, then add 1 Tbsp. of garlic, Worcestershire sauce, thyme and the tomatoes and cook for one hour. Add the lemon juice, adjust salt and pepper to taste and keep warm.

Cut acorn squash in half and remove the seeds. Sprinkle nutmeg and cinnamon over each half. Wrap in foil and bake at 350° for 1½ hours, until fork tender (do not overcook). Reserve until cool and cut the squash into a fine dice after removing the skin. Cut the Andouille sausage and sauté until lightly brown in butter. Add the remaining onions and garlic and sauté briefly before adding the sliced mushrooms. Deglaze with sherry, add the Orzo pasta, the chicken stock and cook like a risotto. When pasta is al dente, add the squash, adjust for salt and pepper to taste. Keep warm and reserve.

Before grilling the shrimps, marinate them in olive oil, salt, pepper and garlic.

Place the orzo in a ring mold or soup cup and place in the center of the plate. Display five shrimps per serving around the orzo and ladle the sauce over the shrimps.

Serves 8
Preparation Time:
  3 Hours
Preheat oven to 350°

- ½ cup olive oil
- 3 large yellow onions, minced
- 1 large green bell pepper, minced
- 2 ribs of celery, minced
- 4 fresh bay leaves
- 4 Tbsps. garlic, minced
- 3 Tbsps. Worcestershire sauce
- ¼ Tbsp. fresh thyme leaves
- 5 lbs. peeled tomatoes
  Juice from 1 lemon
  Salt and pepper to taste
- 1 acorn squash
- ½ Tbsp. cinnamon
- ½ Tbsp. nutmeg
- 1 lb. Andouille sausage
- 6 Tbsps. butter
- 1½ lbs. shiitake mushrooms, stems removed, sliced
- ½ cup dry sherry
- 1 lb. Orzo pasta
- 2 cups low salt chicken stock
- 40 U-12 shrimps (5 per person)

☆

Almond and Sun-Dried Cranberry Bread Pudding with a Spiced Brandy Crème Anglaise

Serves 8
Preparation Time:
1¾ Hours
(note marinating time)

1 cup sun-dried
  cranberries
1 cup brandy
1 loaf of French bread,
  10 oz.
4 cups milk
2 cups sugar
8 Tbsps. melted butter
4 eggs
2 Tbsps. pure vanilla
  extract
1 cup shredded coconut
1 cup slivered almonds,
  toasted, chopped
1 Tbsp. nutmeg

Crème Anglaise:
6 egg yolks
½ cup brandy
½ cup sugar
1 tsp. cinnamon
2 cups heavy cream

Place the cranberries in a bowl with ½ cup of brandy and marinate for one hour to plump the fruit.

Combine the remaining ingredients in a bowl with the drained cranberries. Pour the mixture (moist but not too soggy) into a 9×12-inch baking dish and bake at 350° in a non-preheated oven for 1¼ hours.

For the crème anglaise: In a double boiler, combine yolks, brandy, sugar and cinnamon. Cook until mixture has thickened. Add the cream and cook until the mixture coats the back of a spoon. Serve warm over the pudding.

☆

Roasted Banana and Yam Sorbet

Roast the yams and bananas until soft and dark. Meanwhile, in a saucepan, make a syrup by mixing the sugar, water, pineapple juice, lemon juice and pectin. Boil sauce for 2 minutes.

In a large mixing bowl, blend together the bananas and yams. Add the syrup, mixing until smooth. Strain through a chinois or sieve and add the vanilla.

Process in an ice cream machine.

Serves 4
Preparation Time:
 50 Minutes
(note freezing time)
Preheat oven to 450°

- 1 lb. yams
- 1 lb. bananas
- ¾ cup sugar
- 1 cup water
- ½ cup unsweetened pineapple juice
- Juice from 1 lemon
- 1¼ tsps. pectin
- ½ tsp. vanilla

☆

THE LANAUX HOUSE

547 Esplanade Avenue
New Orleans, Louisiana 70116
(504) 948-6119
ROOM RATES: $135–$250 (for the Lanaux Suite)

particularly impressive reminder of New Orleans' glory days, the Lanaux House stands on the corner of Charles and Esplanade, an unspoiled heirloom in the Renaissance Revival style.

In 1989, owner Ruth Bodenheimer began accepting guests to offset restoration and operating costs for the 11,000-square-foot residence. One of the city's most ideally situated bed and breakfasts, it consists of four luxurious accommodations. The premier Lanaux Suite, originally the library, is an extravaganza with fourteen-foot ceilings and lofty windows that overlook the French Quarter. The opulent room shares a balcony above the courtyard with the comfy Johnson suite, a shuttered, old-world hideaway with bookcases and a wainscoted dining area. The Enchanted Cottage, a haven for honeymooners, is a sunny retreat with creamy brick walls and its own little patio, splashed by tropical blooms and the soft chatter of a wall fountain. Each room is outfitted with a modern bath, antique linens, kitchen facilities (refrigerators are stocked with the makings for breakfast) and other details, like umbrellas and needlepoint "Do Not Disturb" signs.

Public pleasures such as big-name jazz, world-class restaurants, nightclubs, shops and colorful characters are a few steps away.

Creole Jambalaya

Melt the butter in a heavy saucepan and add the onions and pork. Slowly brown, stirring frequently. When slightly brown, add the ham and the garlic.

Add the thyme, bay leaves, parsley and cloves. Brown 5 minutes longer and add the chaurice.

Brown the chaurice. Add the broth and allow to cook for 10 minutes. When it comes to a boil, add the rice and seasonings to taste.

Boil 30 minutes or until rice is done. Stir to mix ingredients well and serve hot.

* Chaurice is a Creole/Cajun pork sausage that is hot, spicy and full-flavored.

Serves 8
Preparation Time:
  45 Minutes

- 2 Tbsps. butter
- 2 onions, chopped
- 1 lb. fresh pork, cut into ½-inch square pieces
- 1 slice ham, chopped fine
- 2 cloves garlic, minced
- 2 sprigs thyme, minced
- 2 bay leaves
- 2 sprigs parsley, minced
- 2 cloves, finely ground
- 1 doz. fine Chaurice,* cut into small pieces
- 3 qts. beef broth
- 1½ cups rice
- Salt, chile pepper and cayenne to taste

☆

OMNI ROYAL ORLEANS HOTEL

621 rue St. Louis at rue Royal
New Orleans, Louisiana 70140
(800)THEOMNI
(504) 529-5333
ROOM RATES: $134–$1,083 (for the 3-bedroom penthouse)

St. Louis and Royal. On that very special corner of the world stands a world-renowned hotel. The Omni Royal Orleans. This landmark is as much a part of legendary New Orleans as Dixieland jazz. Its unsurpassed location in the heart of the French Quarter offers guests easy access to all the excitement of daytime and nighttime New Orleans.

Excellence shines in every detail, just as every room boasts views of courtyards lush with plants prospering in this tropical setting, of Jackson Square, the Mississippi River, or the rooftops of the Vieux Carré. But be assured, this award-winning hotel has not been judged solely on its location, or even the comfort it affords its guests, but also on the creative cuisine of its kitchens.

Under the direction of Executive Chef Raymond Toups, the award-winning Rib Room, renowned for prime rib, beef specialties, Creole classics, fowl and seafood prepared on giant French rotisseries and the mesquite grill, is open for breakfast, lunch and dinner.

Crawfish Salad

Place egg yolks in a small stainless steel mixing bowl, whisk lightly, then add vinegar and Creole mustard. Continue to mix. Slowly add the oils, a little at a time, until it forms a thin sauce. Add the shallots, garlic and herbs and adjust seasonings with salt and pepper to taste.

Place the spinach leaves on a large oval platter and coat lightly with small amount of dressing.

In a separate mixing bowl, place the crawfish tails and mix lightly with the dressing. Season with salt and pepper.

Arrange the seasoned crawfish tails over the spinach in the center of the platter, decorate with whole crawfish and serve.

Serves 6
Preparation Time:
25 Minutes

- 3 egg yolks
- ¼ cup sherry wine vinegar
- 2 Tbsps. coarse Creole mustard
- ½ cup salad oil
- 2 Tbsps. virgin olive oil
- 2 Tbsps. fresh French shallots, chopped
- ½ tsp. fresh garlic, chopped
- 2 Tbsps. fresh parsley, chopped
- 1 Tbsp. fresh tarragon, chopped
  Sea salt and pepper to taste
- 2 lbs. fresh spinach leaves, washed and dried
- 1½ lbs. cooked crawfish tails, peeled, deveined
  Black pepper, freshly ground
- 6 crawfish, boiled in shells for garnish

★

Shrimp Grand Isle

Serves 6
Preparation Time:
 30 Minutes
Preheat oven to 275°

 36 **extra large Gulf of**
     Mexico shrimp, heads
     removed
  5 **eggs, beaten**
     Salt
     Black pepper, freshly
     ground
  2 **Tbsps. parsley,**
     chopped
  2 **Tbsps. garlic, chopped**
  1 **cup flour**
  1 **cup cooking oil**
     Grand Isle Sauce
     (recipe follows)

Grand Isle Sauce:
  4 **shallots, chopped**
  ¾ **cup white wine**
  ¾ **cup whipping cream**
  1 **lb. unsalted butter at**
     room temperature
     Salt and pepper to
     taste
  1 **Tbsp. garlic**
  1 **Tbsp. parsley, chopped**
  2 **lemons, juiced**

Peel and clean the shrimp by cutting through the underside and deveining, leaving the back intact.

Beat eggs lightly and add salt, pepper, parsley and garlic.

Dredge the shrimp in the flour and then in the seasoned egg batter.

Pan fry the shrimp in oil over medium-high heat, turning once. Remove from oil and repeat the process until all the shrimp are cooked. Hold in a 275° oven until ready to serve.

Serve the sauce over the shrimp.

Grand Isle Sauce
Put the shallots and white wine in the saucepan and cook over high heat until reduced by 80 percent. Add the cream and reduce again until the sauce starts to thicken. Whip in the butter and finish with salt, pepper, garlic, parsley and lemon juice.

Fillet of Gulf of Mexico Fish Seared in a Fresh Herb Crust

Season fish with salt and pepper, thyme, tarragon, basil and chives, coating well on both sides.

Heat ¼ cup olive oil in a heavy nonstick fry pan over medium heat and add the fish fillets. Cook 3 to 4 minutes until a nice brown crust forms, turn and finish for 2 minutes or until done. Remove from the pan and keep warm.

Add ¼ cup olive oil to a sauté pan and sauté the peppers and onion for 3 to 4 minutes over high heat. Add the eggplant and garlic and continue to cook for 3 to 4 minutes or until done. Season with salt, pepper and a pinch of the herb mixture used to coat the fish if desired. Vegetables should be soft.

Arrange the eggplant and peppers on a serving plate and place herb-crusted fish on top.

Serves 6
Preparation Time:
  30 Minutes

- 6 fish fillets, (red snapper, grouper, speckled trout or redfish)
  Salt and ground black pepper
- 1 Tbsp. fresh thyme, chopped
- 2 Tbsps. fresh tarragon, chopped
- 2 Tbsps. fresh basil, chopped
- 2 Tbsps. fresh chives, chopped
- ½ cup extra virgin olive oil
- 1 cup red, yellow and green peppers, diced
- ½ cup onion, diced
- 1 cup eggplant, diced
- 2 tsps. fresh garlic, chopped

☆

ROYAL SONESTA HOTEL

300 Bourbon Street
New Orleans, Louisiana 70140
1-800-SONESTA
(504) 586-0300
ROOM RATES: $165–$295

The Royal Sonesta Hotel is a Bourbon Street landmark. Sonesta encompasses almost an entire block, bounded by Bourbon, Conti, Royal and Bienville streets. Traditional Spanish-and French-style architecture, a hidden courtyard, pool patio and wrought-iron lace balconies combine to make this an elegant four-star hotel in the heart of the French Quarter. New Orleans is quite literally at your doorstep.

Housed in the Royal Sonesta is another New Orleans landmark—Begue's Restaurant—world-renowned for its excellent seafood and Creole specialties. You will also find a streetside bistro and oyster bar named Desire, live entertainment in the Mystick Den and the Can Can Café, and Le Booze—a favorite with locals.

Tomato-Tasso Soup

Heat the olive oil in a large stock pot. Add the onions, celery, carrots and garlic. Gently sauté until the vegetables are translucent. Add the tasso, sausage, bay leaves and thyme. Add tomato juice and stock and bring to a boil. Reduce heat and simmer 30 to 40 minutes or until the vegetables are cooked.

Purée the mixture in a food processor, then pass through a strainer and return to the stock pot. Bring to a boil and, while stirring, add cream and butter. Mix well.

Taste and adjust seasonings. Garnish with reserved smoked sausage, sour cream and chives.

Cooking Secret: The tasso has plenty of salt and pepper, so it is highly recommended you taste the soup before adding additional seasonings.

Serves 8
Preparation Time:
  1¼ Hours

4 **Tbsps. olive oil**
4 **onions, diced**
1 **bunch celery, chopped**
2 **carrots, diced**
4 **cloves garlic, peeled and chopped**
1¼ **lbs. tasso, diced**
¾ **lb. smoked sausage, diced (reserve small amount for garnish)**
4 **bay leaves**
2 **sprigs fresh thyme**
1 **can V8 or tomato juice, 48 oz.**
8 **cups chicken stock**
2 **cups heavy cream**
8 **Tbsps. (1 stick) butter**
  Salt and pepper to taste
  Sour cream and chives for garnish

☆

WINDSOR COURT HOTEL

300 Gravier Street
New Orleans, Louisiana 70130
(800) 262-2662
(504) 523-6000
ROOM RATES: $250–$650

I n the center of New Orleans' business district, only four blocks from its famous French Quarter, stands this gracious, award-winning contemporary hotel. Furnished and decorated throughout in traditional style, the elegant decor is complemented by European arts and antiques, including works by Reynolds, Gainsborough and Huysman.

All deluxe guest rooms have a dressing room adjoining the bedroom and bathroom, television, soundproofed walls and top-of-the-line safety measures including smoke detectors and sprinklers. The suites offer a separate living room, a compact kitchen and bay windows overlooking the Mississippi River or the city of New Orleans.

Dining at the Windsor Court Hotel has quickly attracted the attention of those who appreciate fine food and wine, offering a choice of menus, complemented by impeccable service. Executive Chef Jeff Tunks creates an international menu that has made him one of "the best of the best." The wine cellar is one of the finest in the United States.

Macadamia Nut Crusted Halibut with Mango Lime Sauce

I n a saucepan over low heat, combine the mango with the white wine and honey. Reduce to ¼ liquid. Add the cream and reduce further. Place in a blender and purée. Strain. Season with salt and lime juice. Reserve.

Mix the bread crumbs and macadamia nuts in a bowl.

Dip the halibut in the egg and then dip in the bread crumb-macadamia nut mixture. Pan sauté in olive oil until golden brown. Finish in the oven for 3 to 5 minutes.

In sesame oil stir fry the black sesame seeds.

Place a pool of the mango sauce on a plate and top with the halibut. Garnish with snow peas, black sesame seeds and lime wedges.

Serves 4
Preparation Time:
 45 Minutes
Preheat oven to 350°

- 2 mangos, skinned, seeded
- ¾ cup white wine
- 2 Tbsps. honey
- 1 cup cream
- 1 cup fresh bread crumbs
- ½ cup macadamia nuts, chopped
- 2 lbs. halibut
- 4 eggs, beaten
- 4 Tbsps. olive oil
- 1 Tbsp. sesame oil
- 1 tsp. black sesame seeds
- ⅓ lb. snow peas, steamed
- 2 lime wedges, garnish

☆

Louisiana Cooking

Louisiana Culinary History

A **Creole,** by definition, is a person of French or Spanish ancestry born in the New World. However, Creole is also a word of elastic implications, and in culinary terms, Creole refers to a distinctive cuisine indigenous to New Orleans that has its roots in European dishes, enhanced by the liberal use of local seasonings such as filé. The French influence is also strong, but the essence of Creole is in sauces, herbs and the prominent use of seafood.

Cajun cuisine was brought from Nova Scotia to the bayou country by the Acadians more than 250 years ago. Cajun cooks generally use less expensive ingredients than their Creole counterparts, and they are heavy-handed on the herbs and spices. Cajun cuisine is rarely served in its purest form; rather it is often blended with Creole to create what's known as "New Orleans' style" cooking. There is a difference, though, between the two: Creole is distinguished by its rich and heavy sauces; Cajun, by its tendency to be spicy and hot.

In recent years the term **Nouvelle Creole** has been popularized by local restaurateurs. Instead of gumbo or jambalaya, a nouvelle menu might include hickory-grilled items, seafood served with pasta, or smoked meats and fish. There has also been a strong Italian influence in Creole cuisine on the last decade, creating yet another marriage of styles.

Louisiana Cooking Schools

Culinary Arts Institute of Louisiana
427 Lafayette Street
Baton Rouge, Louisiana 70802
800 927-0839, 504 343-6233; Fax 504 336-4880
http://www.caila.com or email: chef@caila.com

Creole Delicacies Cookin' Cajun Cooking School
Store 116 Riverwalk
#1 Pondras Street
New Orleans, Louisiana 70130
800 523-6425, 504 523-6425

Cookin' on the River
600 Decatur, 4th Level
Jackson Brewery Millhouse
New Orleans, Louisiana 70130
800 850-3008, 504 525-2525

New Orleans School of Cooking
620 Decatur Street
New Orleans, Louisiana 70130
800 237-4841, 504 525-2665

Cuisine Éclairée École de Cuisine
The House on Bayou Road
2275 Bayou Road
New Orleans, Louisiana 70119
504 949-7711

Glossary of Terms

Aïoli—strongly flavored garlic mayonnaise from the Provence region of southern France. It is a popular accompaniment for fish, meats and vegetables.

Andouille *(an-dooey)*—Cajun sausage made with pork blade meat, onion, smoked flavorings and garlic. Essential to many Cajun and Creole dishes.

Bain-Marie—a French cooking technique also known as a water bath. It consists of placing a container (pan, bowl, soufflé dish, etc.) of food in a large, shallow pan of warm water, which surrounds the food with gentle heat. The food may be cooked in this manner either in an oven or on top of a range. This technique is designed to cook delicate dishes such as custards, sauces and savory mousses without breaking or curdling them. It can also be used to keep cooked foods warm.

Bananas Foster—a dessert of bananas sautéed with butter, brown sugar and cinnamon, flambéed in white rum and banana liqueur served on ice cream.

Barbecue—Southerners use this term to refer to meat or poultry that has slowly cooked by the smoke of smoldering coals. Foods that are seared quickly over a much hotter fire are "grilled."

Beignet *(ben-yay)*—A French donut without the hole, sprinkled with powdered sugar. A New Orleans tradition with strong coffee.

Béarnaise *(bay-ar-nayz)*—a rich sauce of egg yolk and butter, flavored with tarragon and used on meats and fish.

Bisque—a thick, heartily seasoned soup most often made with crawfish, crab or shrimp. Cream appears in most French versions.

Boudin *(boo-dan)*—hot, spicy pork with onions, rice and herbs, stuffed in sausage casing.

Bouillabaisse *(booey-yah-base)*—a creole bouillabaisse is a stew of various fish and shellfish in a broth seasoned with saffron and often more assertive spices.

Bread Pudding—in the traditional version, stale French bread is soaked in a custard mix, combined with raisins, and baked, then served with a hot, sugary sauce flavored with whiskey or rum.

Café au Lait—a blend, often half and half, of strong coffee and scalded milk.

Café Brûlot *(broo-loh)*—cinnamon, lemon, clove, orange and sugar are steeped with strong coffee, then flambéed with brandy and served in special pedestaled cups.

Chaurice—a Creole/Cajun pork sausage that is hot, spicy and full-flavored, used in cooking both as a main meat dish and in numerous dishes such as gumbos and jambalayas.

Chicory Coffee—A root that is roasted and ground to flavor Louisiana coffee, lending an added bitterness to the taste.

Crème Brûlé *(broo-lay)*—literally, "burned cream." A cream custard with a crust of oven-browned sugar.

Cochon de Lait—a gathering to roast a pig over a blazing fire.

Court-Bouillon *(coo-bee-yon)*—a thick, hearty soup made with a roux, vegetables and fish, served over rice.

Crabs—Lump crab meat from the body of blue crabs in their hard-shell state is excellent for salads, seafood cocktails and crab cakes. When blue crabs molt, they are sold as fully edible soft-shell crabs. Stone crabs are a large, orange-red seasonal delicacy, served as either a first course or an entrée.

Crawfish—also known as crayfish and "mud-bugs" because they live in the mud of freshwater streams. They resemble miniature lobsters and are served in a great variety of ways.

Creole Mustard—Piquant, light brown mustard made from spicy brown mustard seeds.

Dirty Rice—a cousin of jambalaya, a Cajun specialty where cooked rice is combined with bits of meat, such as giblets or sausage, and seasonings, giving the rice a "dirty" look but delicious flavor.

Étouffée *(ay-too-fay)*—crawfish étouffée is made with a butter and flour roux of celery and onion, then cooked for a short period of time and served over rice. Shrimp étouffée is heartier, made with an oil and flour roux or tomato paste, celery, onion, bell pepper, tomatoes and chicken stock, cooked for approximately an hour and served over rice.

Filé *(fee-lay)*—ground sassafras leaves, used to season gumbo and many other Creole specialties.

Grillades *(gree-yads)*—bite-size pieces of veal rounds or beef chuck, braised in red wine, beef stock, garlic, herbs and seasoning, served for brunch with grits and with rice for dinner.

Grits—grains of dried corn that have been ground and hulled, grits are a staple of the Southern breakfast table. They are most frequently served with butter and salt or redeye gravy.

Gulf Fish—red snapper, grouper, speckled trout, redfish, flounder or black drum may be used in recipes that call for gulf fish.

Gumbo—a hearty soup prepared in a variety of combinations such as okra gumbo, shrimp gumbo and chicken gumbo, to name a few.

Hush Puppies—fried balls of cornmeal, often served as a side dish with seafood.

Jambalaya *(jum-bo-lie-yah)*—a spicy rice dish cooked with stock and chopped seasonings, made with any number of ingredients, including sausage, shrimp, ham and chicken.

Jerk seasoning—a dry seasoning blend that originated in the Caribbean islands, and is made of chiles, thyme, cinnamon, ginger, allspice, cloves, garlic and onions. This seasoning is available in the gourmet section or at specialty food stores.

Meunière *(muhn-yehr)*—a method of preparing fish or soft-shell crab by dusting it with seasoned flour, sautéing it in brown butter and using the butter with lemon juice as a sauce. Some restaurants add a dash of Worcestershire sauce.

Mirliton *(merl-i-tawn)*—a pale green member of the squash family usually identified as a vegetable pear. The standard preparation is to scrape the pulp from halved mirlitons, fill them with shrimp and seasoned bread crumbs and bake them.

Muffaletta *(moo-fa-lotta)*—a large, round sandwich containing a combination of thinly sliced cheese, ham and salami, smothered in a heavy, garlicky "olive salad" (a chopped mixture of green olives, pimentos, celery, garlic, onions, capers and spices).

Old Bay Seasoning—A staple seasoning consisting of celery salt, mustard, pepper, cloves and other seasonings.

Oysters Bienville—oysters lightly baked in their shells under a cream sauce flavored with bits of shrimp, mushroom and green seasonings. Some chefs also use garlic or mustard.

Oysters Rockefeller—baked oysters on the half shell in a sauce of puréed aromatic greens laced with anise liqueur. The definitive version is served at Antoine's, where the dish was created with a recipe that is still a secret. Most other restaurants make do with spinach.

Panéed *(pan-aid)*—a cooking method of breading and sautéing in butter.

Po' Boy—a hefty sandwich made with local French bread and any number of fillings: Roast beef, fried shrimp, oysters, ham, meatballs in tomato sauce and cheese are common. A po' boy "dressed" contains lettuce, tomato and mayonnaise or mustard.

Praline *(praw-line)*—candy patty most commonly made from sugar, water or butter and pecans. There are many different flavors and kinds.

Ravigote *(rah-vee-gote)*—in Creole usage, a piquant mayonnaise, usually with capers, used to moisten cold lumps of blue crab meat.

Rémoulade—a cold dressing that accompanies shrimp and sometimes crab meat over shredded lettuce, made of mayonnaise and Creole mustard, oil and vinegar, horseradish, paprika, celery and green onion.

Roux—a mixture of flour and fat that, after being slowly cooked over low heat, is used to thicken mixtures such as soups and sauces. There are three classic roux—white, blond and brown. The color and flavor is determined by the length of time the mixture is cooked. Both white and blond roux are made with butter. The fuller-flavored brown roux can be made with butter or drippings of pork or beef fat. It is cooked to a deep golden brown and used for rich, dark soups and bases. Cajun and Creole dishes use a lard-based roux, which is cooked (sometimes for almost an hour) until it is a beautiful, mahogany brown. This nutty-flavored base is indispensable for specialties like gumbo.

Smothering—a multipurpose Cajun technique that works wonders with everything from game to snap beans. It is similar to braising, where ingredients are briefly browned or sautéed then cooked with a little liquid over heat for a long time. The result is a tender, satisfying dish that makes its own gravy. Other game and poultry that work well this way are squirrel, rabbit, hen and quail.

Soufflée Potatoes—thin, hollow puffs of deep-fried potato. Two fryings at different temperatures produce the puffs.

Tabasco—a very hot, small red pepper originally from the Mexican state of Tabasco. The peppers are fermented in barrels for 3 years before being processed into the sauce. Tabasco Sauce adds zest to numerous dishes.

Tasso—a lean chunk of cured pork, usually a shoulder, or beef that's been richly seasoned with ingredients such as red pepper, garlic, filé powder and any of several other herbs or spices. It's then smoked for about 2 days. The result is a firm, smoky and flavorfully tangy meat that is principally used for seasoning.

Mail Order Sources

 f you are unable to locate some of the specialty food products used in *Louisiana's Cooking Secrets,* you can order them from the mail order sources listed below. The listing is arranged according to their unique specialties.

FISH AND SHELLFISH

Pickwick Catfish Farm
Highway 57
Counce, Tennessee 38326
901-689-3805
Smoked catfish

Joe's Stone Crab Restaurant
Take Away
227 Biscayne Street
Miami Beach, Florida 33139
800-780-CRAB or 305-673-4611
Stone crabs

Handy Soft Shell Crawfish
10557 Cherry Hill Avenue
Baton Rouge, Louisiana 70816
504-292-4552
Soft-shell crawfish

Vieux Carré Foods, Inc.
P.O. Box 50277
New Orleans, Louisiana 70510
504-822-6065
Shrimp and crab boil

GRITS

Adams Milling Company
Route 6, Box 148A
Napier Field Station
Dothan, Alabama 36303
205-983-4233
Grits milled from whole-kernel corn

Hopping John's
30 Pinckney Street
Charleston, South Carolina
   29401
803-577-6404
Stone-ground cornmeal, grits and corn flour

RICE

Konriko Company Store
P.O. Box 10640
New Iberia, Louisiana
   70562-0640
800-551-3245
Wild pecan rice

SAUSAGES

Aidells Sausage Company
1575 Minnesota Street
San Francisco, California 94107
415-285-6660
Andouille and other varieties of sausage

Baltz Brothers
1612 Elm Hill Pike
Nashville, Tennessee 37210
615-360-3100
Hickory-smoked sausage and bacon

Comeaux's Grocery
1000 Lamar Street
Lafayette, Louisiana 70501
800-323-2492 or 800-737-2666
Boudin blanc and boudin rouge sausage

SEASONINGS AND SAUCES

K-Paul's Louisiana Mail Order
824 Distributors Row
P.O. Box 23342
New Orleans, Louisiana
   70183-0342
800-457-2857
Seasoning blends, cookbooks, videos, cast-iron skillets, jellies and Louisiana grown rice

Louisiana General Store
The Jackson Brewery
620 Decatur Street
New Orleans, Louisiana 70130
800-237-4841
Filé powder and many more ingredients for Cajun and Creole cuisines

Exclusively Barbecue
P.O. Box 3048
Concord, North Carolina 28025
800-948-1009
Barbecue sauces and grills

Tabasco Country Store
McIlhenny Company
Avery Island, Louisiana
   70513-5002
800-634-9599
Tabasco® brand hot pepper sauce and other products

Trappey's Fine Foods, Inc.
P.O. Box 13610
New Iberia, Louisiana
   70562-3610
800-365-8727 or 318-365-8727
Hot sauces

SWEET ONIONS

Bland Farms
P.O. Box 506
Glennville, Georgia 30427-0506
800-843-2542
Vidalia onions and baby Vidalias

Planters Three
P.O. Box 92
Wadmalaw Island, South
   Carolina 29412
800-772-6732
Wadmalaw sweet onions

SYRUP

C.S. Steen Syrup Mill, Inc.
P.O. Box 339
Abbeville, Louisiana 70510
318-893-7654
Cane syrup

COFFEE AND TEA

Charleston Tea Plantation
6617 Maybank Highway
Wadmalaw Island,
   South Carolina 29487
800-443-5987
American Classic tea

Community Kitchens
P.O. Box 2311
Baton Rouge, Louisiana
   70821-2311
800-535-9901 or 504-381-3900
Community coffee, Creole mustard and Louisiana specialties

The Company Store
1039 Decatur Street
New Orleans, Louisiana 70116
504-581-2914
Café du Monde coffee

Recipe Index

About the Author

KATHLEEN DEVANNA FISH, author of the popular "Secrets" series, is a gourmet cook and gardener who is always on the lookout for recipes with style and character.

In addition to *Louisiana's Cooking Secrets*, Kathleen has written the award-winning *Great Vegetarian Cookbook, Cooking Secrets From America's South, Pacific Northwest Cooking Secrets, Cooking Secrets for Healthy Living, The Gardener's Cookbook, The Great California Cookbook, California Wine Country Cooking Secrets, San Francisco's Cooking Secrets, Monterey's Cooking Secrets, New England's Cooking Secrets, Cape Cod's Cooking Secrets* and *Cooking and Traveling Inn Style*.

Before embarking on a writing and publishing career, she owned and operated three businesses in the travel and hospitality industry.

ROBERT FISH, award-winning photojournalist, produces the images that bring together the concept of the "Secrets" series.

In addition to taking the cover photographs, Robert explores the food and wine of each region, helping to develop the overview upon which each book is based.

Bon Vivant Press

A division of The Millennium Publishing Group

PO Box 1994 • Monterey, CA 93942

800-524-6826 • 408-373-0592 • FAX 408-373-3567 • http://www.millpub.com

Send _____ copies of *Cooking with the Masters of Food & Wine* at $34.95 each.

Send _____ copies of *The Elegant Martini* at $17.95 each.

Send _____ copies of *Cooking Secrets from Around the World* at $15.95 each.

Send _____ copies of *Cooking Secrets from America's South* at $15.95 each.

Send _____ copies of *Louisiana's Cooking Secrets* at $15.95 each.

Send _____ copies of *Pacific Northwest Cooking Secrets* at $15.95 each.

Send _____ copies of *Cooking Secrets for Healthy Living* at $15.95 each.

Send _____ copies of *The Great California Cookbook* at $15.95 each.

Send _____ copies of *The Gardener's Cookbook* at $15.95 each.

Send _____ copies of *The Great Vegetarian Cookbook* at $15.95 each.

Send _____ copies of *California Wine Country Cooking Secrets* at $14.95 each.

Send _____ copies of *San Francisco's Cooking Secrets* at $13.95 each.

Send _____ copies of *Monterey's Cooking Secrets* at $13.95 each.

Send _____ copies of *New England's Cooking Secrets* at $14.95 each.

Send _____ copies of *Cape Cod's Cooking Secrets* at $14.95 each.

Send _____ copies of *Jewish Cooking Secrets From Here and Far* at $14.95 each.

Send _____ copies of *Pets Welcome California* at $15.95 each.

Send _____ copies of *Pets Welcome America's South* at $15.95 each.

Add $4.50 postage and handling for the first book ordered and $1.50 for each additional book. Please add $1.08 sales tax per book, for those books shipped to California addresses.

Please charge my ☐ Visa
☐ MasterCard   # _____

Expiration date_____Signature _____

Enclosed is my check for _____

Name _____

Address _____

City_____State_____Zip _____

☐ This is a gift. Send directly to:

Name _____

Address _____

City_____State_____Zip _____

☐ Autographed by the author
   Autographed to _____